CONTI

Copyright © 2020 by *Nazarene Books*. ISBN 978-1-64106-066-0. Booklet produced for the: *Continuing* Church of God and Successor, a corporation sole. 1036 W. Grand Avenue, Grover Beach, California, 93433 USA.

Scriptural quotes are mostly taken from the New King James Version (Thomas Nelson, Copyright © 1997; used by permission) sometimes abbreviated as NKJV, but normally shown without any abbreviation.

1. God's Plan is a Mystery to Most

The Bible teaches:

> [1] In the beginning God created the heavens and the earth. (Genesis 1:1, NKJV throughout unless otherwise indicated)

But why?

What is the meaning of life?

Throughout the ages people have wondered if there is a purpose being worked out on the earth.

And if there is, what is it?

Presuming there is a God, why did He make anything?

Why did God create humans? Why did God make you?

Does your life have any purpose?

Different cultures and different religions have their views. But are they consistent with the Bible?

What is the truth?

Part of the truth is that God's plan is a mystery to most. Notice something that the Bible teaches about that:

> [25] Now to Him who is able to establish you according to my gospel and the preaching of Jesus Christ, according to **the revelation of the mystery kept secret since the world began** [26] **but now made manifest, and by the prophetic Scriptures** made known to all nations, according to the commandment of the everlasting God, for obedience to the faith — [27] to God, alone wise, be glory through Jesus Christ forever. Amen. (Romans 16:25-27)

The Bible tells of the mystery which has been kept secret since the world began, but that it is revealed in prophetic scriptures—"the word of truth" (2 Timothy 2:15; James 1:18).

The Bible refers to many mysteries, such as the mystery of the kingdom of God (Mark 4:11), the mystery of grace (Ephesians 3:1-5), the mystery of faith (1 Timothy 3:9), the mystery of the marriage relationship (Ephesians 5:28-33), the mystery of lawlessness (2 Thessalonians 2:7), the mystery of the resurrection (1 Corinthians 15:51-54), the mystery of Christ (Ephesians 3:4) the mystery of the Father (Colossians 2:2), the mystery of God (Colossians 2:2; Revelation 10:7) and even Mystery Babylon the Great (Revelation 17:5).

Although this may come as a surprise to many, the three writers of the synoptic Gospels all recorded that Jesus did not speak in parables so that people would better understand. They recorded that Jesus said He spoke in parables to keep mysteries of the Kingdom of God unknown for many (Matthew 13:11; Mark 4:11-12; Luke 8:10) in this age.

The Apostle Paul wrote that faithful ministers are the "stewards of the mysteries of God" (1 Corinthians 4:1; cf. 13:2) who are to be "speaking the truth in love" (Ephesians 4:15).

Are you interested in knowing more about many of the mysteries that the Bible tells of?

Do you want to know why God made anything?

Would you like to know why God made you?

Yes, many have their own ideas.

Is there a way for YOU to really know?

Those who are willing to believe the Bible over human traditions can know.

However, since many of even the most basic aspects of God's plan are a mystery to most, please take the time to read the entire book, and as you wish, to look up some of the scriptures that are just cited (as opposed to being fully quoted) for even more clarification.

The mysteries can be made known by understanding the prophetic scriptures for those obedient in faith.

Yet they have not been made known to all in this age, only to those now called:

> [11] ... "To you it has been given to know the mystery of the kingdom of God; but to those who are outside, all things come in parables" (Mark 4:11)

> [25] For I do not desire, brethren, that you should be ignorant of this mystery, lest you should be wise in your own opinion, that blindness in part has happened to Israel until the fullness of the Gentiles has come in. (Romans 11:25)

> [7] But we speak the wisdom of God in a mystery, the hidden wisdom which God ordained before the ages for our glory, (1 Corinthians 2:7)

For more specifically on the "mystery of the kingdom of God" and the "mystery of the gospel" (Ephesians 6:19), you can also check out our free booklet *The Gospel of the Kingdom of God*. Related to "the fullness of the Gentiles", check out the free book *Universal OFFER of Salvation, Apokatastasis: Can God save the lost in an age to come? Hundreds of scriptures reveal God's plan of salvation*. Both are available online at www.ccog.org.

The Apostle Paul wrote:

> [8] To me, who am less than the least of all the saints, this grace was given, that I should preach among the Gentiles the unsearchable riches of Christ, [9] and to make all see what is the fellowship of the mystery, which from the beginning of the ages has been hidden in God who created all things through Jesus Christ; [10] to the intent that now the manifold wisdom of God might be made known by the church to the principalities and

4

powers in the heavenly places, [11] according to the eternal purpose which He accomplished in Christ Jesus our Lord, [12] in whom we have boldness and access with confidence through faith in Him. (Ephesians 3:8-12)

[25] ... I became a minister according to the stewardship from God which was given to me for you, to fulfill the word of God, [26] the mystery which has been hidden from ages and from generations, but now has been revealed to His saints. [27] To them God willed to make known what are the riches of the glory of this mystery among the Gentiles: which is Christ in you, the hope of glory. (Colossians 1:25-27)

There are many "riches" that are "unsearchable" without the word of God. These are essentially biblical mysteries that have long been hidden.

In the 2nd century, Bishop/Pastor Polycarp of Smyrna wrote of "the prophetic mystery of the coming of Christ" (Polycarp, Fragments from Victor of Capua. Translated by Stephen C. Carlson, 2006; details about mysteries concerning His coming can be found in the free online book, available at www.ccog.org, titled: *Proof Jesus is the Messiah*).

Also, in the 2nd century, Bishops/Pastors Ignatius and Melito wrote that the ministry understood about various scriptural mysteries (e.g. Ignatius' *Epistle to the Ephesians*; Melito's *Homily on the Passover*).

Jesus and the Apostles explained some of these mysteries to those who became early Christians. We in the *Continuing* Church of God strive to do that now for those who are willing to look.

The Nature of God

Understanding a bit about the nature of God will help us better understand the mysteries of His plan.

The Bible teaches "God is love" (1 John 4:16), "God is Spirit" (John 4:24), "Yahweh is good" (Nahum 1:7, World English Bible), all-powerful

(Jeremiah 32:17,27), all-knowing (Isaiah 46:9-10), and that He is eternal (Isaiah 57:15).

The Apostle Paul wrote:

> [7] In Him we have redemption through His blood, the forgiveness of sins, according to the riches of His grace [8] which He made to abound toward us in all wisdom and prudence, [9] having made known to us the mystery of His will, according to His good pleasure which He purposed in Himself, [10] that in the dispensation of the fullness of the times He might gather together in one all things in Christ, both which are in heaven and which are on earth — in Him. (Ephesians 1:7-10)

Notice that God's will is a mystery to most (those not now called), essentially until the dispensation of the fullness of times—which will come for most after a prophesied resurrection.

Yet, God long ago laid out aspects of His plan:

> [11] The counsel of the Lord stands forever, The plans of His heart to all generations. (Psalm 33:11)

> [18] knowing that you were not redeemed with corruptible things, like silver or gold, from your aimless conduct received by tradition from your fathers, [19] but with the precious blood of Christ, as of a lamb without blemish and without spot. [20] He indeed was foreordained before the foundation of the world, but was manifest in these last times for you. (1 Peter 1:18-20)

> [8] All who dwell on the earth will worship him {the beast}, whose names have not been written in the Book of Life of the Lamb slain from the foundation of the world. (Revelation 13:8)

The fact that the Bible says that the Lamb, meaning Jesus (cf. John 1:29, 36), was intended to be slain from the beginning shows that God knew humans would sin and He has long had a plan.

The prophet Isaiah was inspired to record this about the certainty of God's plan:

> [8] "Remember this, and show yourselves men; Recall to mind, O you transgressors. [9] Remember the former things of old, For I am God, and there is no other; I am God, and there is none like Me, [10] Declaring the end from the beginning, And from ancient times things that are not yet done, Saying, 'My counsel shall stand, And I will do all My pleasure,' [11] Calling a bird of prey from the east, The man who executes My counsel, from a far country. Indeed I have spoken it; I will also bring it to pass. I have purposed it; I will also do it. (Isaiah 46:8-11)

> [11] The counsel of the Lord stands forever, The plans of His heart to all generations. (Psalm 33:11)

God's plans will come to pass.

Consider also the following:

> [16] For God so loved the world that He gave His only begotten Son, that whoever believes in Him should not perish but have everlasting life. [17] **For God did not send His Son into the world to condemn the world, but that the world through Him might be saved** (John 3:16-17).

Now that we see some of God's attributes, such as He is good, is a planner, and is love: this should help us better understand Him and His basic motivations as to why He made anything.

You are important. You matter! God loves YOU personally. And does have a plan for you personally.

2. Why the Creation? Why Humans? Why Satan? What is Truth? What are the Mysteries of Rest and Sin?

One of the biggest questions that philosophers have had throughout the ages is, "Why are we here?" Another is, "Why is there anything?"

The basic answers to these questions can be found in the word of God, the Bible.

While there are various ideas about the origins of the universe, there is a consensus among many scientists, as well as religious people, that human beings all had the same mother (though there are disputes as to how far back that goes).

The Book of Genesis

We get some ideas about why God created anything in the first book of the Bible, commonly known as Genesis.

Repeatedly the Book of Genesis shows that God saw what He made was good (Genesis 1:4,10,12,18, 21, 25, 31). And, the later Book of Isaiah informs us that God formed the earth to be inhabited (Isaiah 45:18).

Genesis teaches this regarding God making humans:

> [26] Then God said, "Let Us make man in Our image, according to Our likeness; let them have dominion over the fish of the sea, over the birds of the air, and over the cattle, over all the earth and over every creeping thing that creeps on the earth."

> [27] So God created man in His own image; in the image of God He created him; male and female He created them. [28] Then God blessed them, and God said to them, "Be fruitful and multiply; fill the earth and subdue it; have dominion over the fish of the sea, over the birds of the air, and over every living thing that moves on the earth."

²⁹ And God said, "See, I have given you every herb that yields seed which is on the face of all the earth, and every tree whose fruit yields seed; to you it shall be for food. ³⁰ Also, to every beast of the earth, to every bird of the air, and to everything that creeps on the earth, in which there is life, I have given every green herb for food"; and it was so. (Genesis 1:26-30)

God formed humans after the God kind, not after an animal kind. God is essentially reproducing Himself (Malachi 2:15). We see that humans were created in a somewhat physical image of God to rule over things on the earth (cf. Hebrews 2:5-8), and other scriptures show that deification is part of the plan (cf. 1 John 3:2).

Were humans and the creation bad?

No. The next verse in Genesis tells us:

³¹ Then God saw everything that He had made, and indeed it was very **good**. So the evening and the morning were the sixth day. (Genesis 1:31)

So, the entire re-creation (Genesis 1:3-2:3) was very good and, as it would seem, so would be God's instructions for humans to subdue the earth (Genesis 1:28).

After the sixth day, God rested:

¹ Thus the heavens and the earth, and all the host of them, were finished. ² And on the seventh day God ended His work which He had done, and He rested on the seventh day from all His work which He had done. ³ Then God blessed the seventh day and sanctified it, because in it He rested from all His work which God had created and made. (Genesis 2:1-3)

God, in essence, made a physical creation in six days and a more spiritual creation on the seventh.

God blessing the seventh day also shows that He considered it "good" (in Exodus 20:8, He says to "keep it holy").

God has a plan.

What is Man?

Notice also the following from Genesis:

> 15 Then the Lord God took the man and put him in the garden of Eden to tend and keep it. (Genesis 2:15)

The reason to tend and keep the garden was to work to make it better.

The Old Testament teaches:

> 4 What is man that You are mindful of him,
> And the son of man that You visit him?
> 5 For You have made him a little lower than the angels,
> And You have crowned him with glory and honor.
>
> 6 You have made him to have dominion over the works of Your hands;
> You have put all things under his feet,
> 7 All sheep and oxen —
> Even the beasts of the field,
> 8 The birds of the air,
> And the fish of the sea
> That pass through the paths of the seas. (Psalm 8:4-8)

Humans were given dominion over the earth (part of the works of God's hands). The New Testament amplifies this even further:

> 5 For He has not put the world to come, of which we speak, in subjection to angels. 6 But one testified in a certain place, saying:
>
> "What is man that You are mindful of him, Or the son of man that You take care of him? 7 You have made him a little lower than the angels; You have crowned him with glory and honor, And set him over the works of Your hands. 8 You have put all things in subjection under his feet."

For in that He put all in subjection under him, He left nothing that is not put under him. But now we do not yet see all things put under him. ⁹ But we see Jesus, who was made a little lower than the angels, for the suffering of death crowned with glory and honor, that He, by the grace of God, might taste death for everyone.

¹⁰ For it was fitting for Him, for whom are all things and by whom are all things, in bringing many sons to glory, to make the captain of their salvation perfect through sufferings. ¹¹ For both He who sanctifies and those who are being sanctified are all of one, for which reason He is not ashamed to call them brethren, ¹² saying:

"I will declare Your name to My brethren; In the midst of the assembly I will sing praise to You."

¹³ And again:

"I will put My trust in Him."

And again:

"Here am I and the children whom God has given Me."

¹⁴ Inasmuch then as the children have partaken of flesh and blood, He Himself likewise shared in the same, that through death He might destroy him who had the power of death, that is, the devil, ¹⁵ and release those who through fear of death were all their lifetime subject to bondage. ¹⁶ For indeed He does not give aid to angels, but He does give aid to the seed of Abraham. ¹⁷ Therefore, in all things He had to be made like His brethren, that He might be a merciful and faithful High Priest in things pertaining to God, to make propitiation for the sins of the people. (Hebrews 2:5-17)

So, ruling the universe is part of the plan.

Yet, one of the reasons that all things are not yet under human control is the following:

> [23] for all have sinned and fall short of the glory of God, (Romans 3:23)

But redeeming us from sin is part of the plan (cf. Romans 3:24-26), so we will later be able to rule.

Mystery of Humans Compared to Animals

Are humans just animals, distinguished only as more highly evolved than other primates?

No.

Scientists have struggled with this.

But those willing to accept God's word could understand.

Humans have the spirit of man in them, whereas animals, including the other primates, do not have that same spirit. The reality that there is a spirit in humans is taught in both the Old and New Testaments:

> [8] But there is a spirit in man, And the breath of the Almighty gives him understanding. (Job 32:8)

> [11] For what man knows the things of a man except the spirit of the man which is in him?... (1 Corinthians 2:11)

Secularists do not want to admit that there is a spirit in man that God gave.

But there is.

And that spirit of man differs from the type of spirit animals have (cf. Ecclesiastes 3:21).

Back in 1978, the old Worldwide Church of God put out a booklet by Herbert W. Armstrong titled *What Science Can't Discover About The Human Mind*. Here are some excerpts from it:

> WHY cannot the greatest minds solve world problems? Scientists have said, "Given sufficient knowledge, and we shall solve all human problems and cure all our evils." Since 1960 the world's fund of knowledge has doubled. But humanity's evils also have doubled. ...
>
> But the greatest human minds have never comprehended that divinely-revealed KNOWLEDGE. It is as if God our Maker had sent his message to us in an unbreakable secret code.
>
> And the greatest human minds have never cracked that secret code. Modern Science cannot understand it. Psychologists do not themselves understand of what the human mind is composed. ...
>
> There is virtually no difference in shape and construction between animal brain and human brain. The brains of elephants, whales, and dolphins are larger than human brain, and the chimp's brain is slightly smaller.
>
> Qualitatively the human brain may be very slightly superior, but not enough to remotely account for the difference in output.
>
> What, then, can account for the vast difference? Science cannot adequately answer. Some scientists, in the field of brain research, conclude that, of necessity, there has to be some nonphysical component in human brain that does not exist in animal brain. But most scientists will not admit the possibility of the existence of the nonphysical.
>
> What other explanation is there? Actually, outside of the very slight degree of physical superiority of human brain, science has NO explanation, due to unwillingness to concede even the possibility of the spiritual.

When man refuses to admit even the very existence of his own Maker, he shuts out of his mind vast oceans of basic true knowledge, fact, and UNDERSTANDING. When he substitutes FABLE for truth, he is, of all men, MOST IGNORANT, though he professes himself to be wise. ...

MAN was made out of the dust of the ground. He receives his temporary human life from air, breathed in and out of his nostrils. His life is in the blood (Gen. 9:4, 6). But the lifeblood is oxidized by breathing air, even as gasoline in the carburetor of an automobile. Therefore breath is the "breath of life" even as the life is in the blood.

Notice carefully that MAN, made wholly of matter, BECAME a living soul as soon as the BREATH gave him his temporary physical life. ... The SOUL is composed of physical MATTER, not Spirit.

I have explained that human brain is almost identical to animal brain. But man was made in the form and shape of God, to have a special relationship with God — to have the potential of being born into the FAMILY of God. And God is SPIRIT (John 4:24). To make it possible to bridge the gap — or to make the transition of MANKIND, composed wholly of MATTER, into SPIRIT beings in God's Kingdom, then to be composed wholly of Spirit, and at the same time to give MAN a MIND like God's — God put a spirit in each human.

In Job 32:8, we read, "There is a spirit in man: and the inspiration of the Almighty giveth them understanding."

This is a great TRUTH, understood by but very few.

I call this spirit the HUMAN spirit, for it is IN each human, even though it is SPIRIT ESSENCE and not matter. It is NOT a spirit person or being. It is not the MAN, but spirit essence IN the man. It is NOT a soul — the physical human is a soul. The human spirit imparts the power of INTELLECT to the human brain.

The human spirit does not supply human LIFE — the human LIFE is in the physical BLOOD, oxidized by the BREATH of life.

It is that nonphysical component in the human brain that does not exist in the brain of animals. It is the ingredient that makes possible the transition from human to divine, without changing matter into spirit, at the time of resurrection. That I will explain a little later.

Let me make clear a few essential points about this spirit in man. It is spirit essence, just as in matter air is essence, and so is water. This human spirit cannot see. The physical BRAIN sees, through the eyes. The human spirit IN a person cannot hear. The brain hears through the ears. This human spirit cannot think.

The brain thinks — although the spirit imparts the power to think, whereas brute animal brains without such spirit cannot, except in the most elementary manner. ...

Just as no dumb animal can know the things of man's knowledge, neither could man, by brain alone, except by the spirit of man — the human spirit — that is in man. So also, in the same manner, even a man cannot know — comprehend — the things of God, unless or until he receives another spirit — the Holy Spirit of GOD.

Stated still another way, all humans have from birth a spirit called "the spirit of man" which is IN THEM. Notice carefully that this spirit is NOT the man. It is something IN THE MAN. A man might swallow a small marble. It is then something in the man, but it is not the man or any part of him as a man. The man was made of the dust of the ground — mortal. This human spirit is not the soul. It is something IN the soul which itself IS the physical MAN.

Notice, further, verse 14: "But the natural man receiveth not the things of the Spirit of God: for they are foolishness unto him; neither can he know them, because they are spiritually discerned."

So, from birth, God gives US one spirit, which for lack of a better term I call a human spirit. It gives us MIND power which is not in animal BRAIN. Yet that MIND power is limited to knowledge of the physical universe. WHY? Because knowledge enters the human mind ONLY through the five physical senses.

But notice that God had not completed the creation of MAN at the creation of Adam and Eve. The physical creation was completed. They had this "human" spirit at their creation. ...

HOW has God planned to "bridge the gap" from physical to spiritual composition — to reproduce Himself out of PHYSICAL HUMANS THAT COME FROM THE PHYSICAL GROUND?

First, God put IN the physical MAN a "human" spirit. It is NOT, however, the human spirit that makes the decisions, comes to repentance, or builds the character. As I have emphasized, this spirit does not impart life, cannot see, hear, feel or think. It empowers the PHYSICAL MAN, through his BRAIN, to do these things. But this spirit RECORDS every thought — every bit of knowledge received through the five senses and it records whatever character — good or bad — that is developed in human life.

The human MAN is made literally from CLAY. God is like the master potter forming and shaping a vessel out of clay. But if the clay is too hard, it will not bend into the form and shape he wants. If it is too soft and moist, it lacks firmness to "STAY PUT" where the potter bends it.

Notice in Isaiah 64:8: "But now, O [ETERNAL], thou art our father; we are the clay, and thou our potter; and we all are the work of thy hand."

Yet God has given each of us a MIND OF HIS OWN. If one REFUSES to acknowledge God or God's ways — refuses to repent of the wrong and turn to the right, God cannot take him and create Godly character in him. But the human CLAY must be pliable, must yield willingly. If the human stiffens up and resists,

16

he is like clay that is too dry and stiff. The potter can do nothing with it. It will not give and bend. Also, if he is so lacking in will, purpose, and determination that he won't "stay put" when God molds him partly into what God wants him to be — too wishy-washy, weak, lacking root of character, he will never endure to the end. He will lose out. ...

It must be GOD'S righteousness, for all of OURS is like filthy rags to Him. He continually instills His knowledge, His righteousness, His character within us — IF we diligently seek it and want it. BUT WE HAVE OUR VERY IMPORTANT PART IN IT. ...

As we receive the CHARACTER OF GOD through the Holy Spirit of God, more and more God is REPRODUCING HIMSELF IN us.

Finally, in the resurrection, we shall be as God — in a position where we cannot sin, because we ourselves have set it so and have turned FROM sin and have struggled and struggled AGAINST sin and overcome sin.

God's PURPOSE WILL be accomplished!

Yes, God's purpose will be accomplished.

Why Did God Make Males and Females?

Related to the creation of humans, why did God make them male and female?

Well, an obvious reason would have to do with reproduction as God told the first man and woman:

> [28] Be fruitful and multiply; fill the earth... (Genesis 1:28).

The Bible gives a fairly specific related reason:

> [14] ... Between you and the wife of your youth ... she is your companion And your wife by covenant. [15] But did He not make

them one, Having a remnant of the Spirit? And why one? He seeks godly offspring... (Malachi 2:14bd-15)

God made males and females so that they could be one and ultimately produce godly offspring (for deification).

Jesus taught:

> [4] And He answered and said to them, "Have you not read that He who made them at the beginning 'made them male and female,' [5] and said, 'For this reason a man shall leave his father and mother and be joined to his wife, and the two shall become one flesh'? [6] So then, they are no longer two but one flesh. Therefore what God has joined together, let not man separate." (Matthew 19:4-6)

The Apostle Paul wrote related to this that, "This is a great mystery, but I speak concerning Christ and the church" (Ephesians 5:32).

In addition, the two properly becoming one also helps us better understand the relationship between the Father and the Son (John 17:20-23).

The marriage relationship helps picture the relationship between the Father and the Son (both of whom the Bible identifies as God, e.g. Colossians 2:2, which is a mystery to most) as well as what will happen to converted humans after the resurrection (which the Bible also calls a mystery, e.g. 1 Corinthians 15:51-54).

The Apostle Paul discussed love and gave some other spiritual lessons related to the marital state:

> [4] ... admonish the young women to love their husbands, to love their children (Titus 2:4).

> [22] Wives, submit to your own husbands, as to the Lord. [23] For the husband is head of the wife, as also Christ is head of the church; and He is the Savior of the body. [24] Therefore, just as

the church is subject to Christ, so let the wives be to their own husbands in everything.

25 Husbands, love your wives, just as Christ also loved the church and gave Himself for her, 26 that He might sanctify and cleanse her with the washing of water by the word, 27 that He might present her to Himself a glorious church, not having spot or wrinkle or any such thing, but that she should be holy and without blemish. (Ephesians 5:22-27)

Another reason to make males and females was to make it possible, though with physical distinctions in this life, for couples to be glorified together with Jesus (Romans 8:16-17). Working together (Genesis 1:28; Ecclesiastes 4:9-12) and even suffering together in this life was also part of the plan (Romans 8:16-17) for male-female couples.

Let's also see some lessons from history:

30 By faith the walls of Jericho fell down after they were encircled for seven days. 31 By faith the harlot Rahab did not perish with those who did not believe, when she had received the spies with peace. 32 And what more shall I say? For the time would fail me to tell of Gideon and Barak and Samson and Jephthah, also of David and Samuel and the prophets: 33 who through faith subdued kingdoms, worked righteousness, obtained promises, stopped the mouths of lions, 34 quenched the violence of fire, escaped the edge of the sword, out of weakness were made strong, became valiant in battle, turned to flight the armies of the aliens. 35 Women received their dead raised to life again. Others were tortured, not accepting deliverance, that they might obtain a better resurrection. 36 Still others had trial of mockings and scourgings, yes, and of chains and imprisonment. 37 They were stoned, they were sawn in two, were tempted, were slain with the sword. They wandered about in sheepskins and goatskins, being destitute, afflicted, tormented — 38 of whom the world was not worthy. They wandered in deserts and mountains, in dens and caves of the earth. 39 And all these, having obtained a good testimony through faith, did not receive the promise, 40 God having

provided something better for us, that they should not **be made perfect** apart from us. (Hebrews 11:30-40)

Both men and women had faith and were heirs to the promises—equally. And both men and women are to be made perfect. And this will be better for us.

For what purpose?

To give love in a unique way throughout all eternity.

As the Apostle Paul wrote to Christians (and not just married couples):

[12] And may the Lord make you **increase and abound in love to one another and to all** ... (1 Thessalonians 3:12)

Whether male or female, humans are intended to give love. Increasing love to all will make eternity better.

What Happened to Humans?

When God first made humans, He blessed them (Genesis 1:28). He also said that all He made (including humans) was "very good" (Genesis 1:31).

Furthermore, notice that the Bible specifically teaches:

[29] ...That God made man upright, But they have sought out many schemes. (Ecclesiastes 7:29)

In the Garden of Eden, God gave the first true humans—Adam and Eve (Genesis 3:20)—everything that they really needed.

They had a clean and pleasant environment, food, and something to do (Genesis 2:8-24). They basically lived by the truth.

But there also is an unseen spirit world that is a mystery to most. There is an unseen realm that includes angels. The Bible shows that before human beings were created a third of angels rebelled and followed an adversary now known as Satan (Revelation 12:4).

In time, Satan (cf. Revelation 12:9) appeared as a serpent. He then told Eve that God was holding back on them (Genesis 3:1,4-5).

The serpent deceived Eve by his craftiness (2 Corinthians 11:3). Satan told Eve to not believe God's word (Genesis 3:2-4). He appealed to Eve's personal lusts and vanity and she chose to disobey God and listen to Satan instead (Genesis 3:6a). Her husband Adam was there with Eve, and decided he should sin and be with her (Genesis 3:6b).

Speculative Insert: Human Longevity

After the first five chapters of the Book of Genesis, where we see some people living over 900 years.

So why did early people like Adam and Noah live so long?

The Jewish historian Josephus claimed that partially this was because God had the food "fitter" for them as well as to give them time to develop early technologies (Antiquities Book 1, 3:9).

Seemingly, however, a reason that God allowed people to live longer lives before was so that they could better see the consequences of sin and living apart from God's ways. Back then, the effects of pollution, for example, would not be as quickly obvious as they are in the 21st century. Furthermore, having longer lifespans would have helped them better see societal and other problems that humans were getting themselves into.

They would see that humans were NOT making the world better. Therefore, after they will be resurrected (Revelation 20:11-12), they would better realize the errors in not going God's way.

Later generations would have seen the Great Flood (it is in the historical records of many societies) as well as seen more of the negative effects of humankind following Satan's direction, as opposed to truly living God's way.

God determined it was better for the later generations to live shorter lives, generally speaking, and suffer for shorter periods. God's plan is to minimize suffering (cf. Lamentations 3:33).

Mystery of Satan and His Demons

But it was not just Eve who was deceived. The New Testament says "that serpent of old" is "called the Devil and Satan, who deceives the whole world" (Revelation 12:9).

Jesus taught that Satan was a liar and the father (originator) of lies (John 8:44).

Originally, Satan was known as Lucifer (Isaiah 14:12), which means "bearer of light." He was a "cherub" (Ezekiel 28:14). A cherub is a winged angelic being whose roles included being at the mercy seat of God (Exodus 25:18-20; Ezekiel 28:14,16).

Lucifer was created as a basically perfect (cf. Ezekiel 28:15) and attractive being (cf. Ezekiel 28:17). But that perfection did not last (Ezekiel 28:15).

God created Lucifer and the angels, but, in a sense, their creation was not complete until character was formed in them. Now God cannot put character instantaneously into one—if He did so, basically He would be creating some type of "computer-controlled" robot. This is true of spirit beings as well as human beings.

If God created righteous character instantaneously by fiat, there wouldn't be any character, because character is that capacity of a separate entity, of the individual, to come to his/her own knowledge of the truth, and to make his/her own decision, and to will to follow the right instead of the wrong. And the individual created must make that decision. In other words, the individual, human or angelic, has a part in his/her/its own creation.

This is a mystery to most as few people have fully understood this.

Please understand that the Bible shows that, well prior to the incident in the Garden of Eden, Satan was "perfect in his ways" (Ezekiel 28:11-15a), but then he succumbed to pride and iniquity and was cast down to the earth (Ezekiel 28:15b-17; Isaiah 14:12-14). He became an adversary of God (Satan means adversary), instead of properly building righteous character.

His rebellion was one reason that after the initial creation of Genesis 1:1, there was chaos and the earth became "desolate" (ISV, GNB) in Genesis 1:2. So God then went to "renew the face of the earth" (Psalm 104:30), which included making things He did during the "re-creation" (Genesis 1:3-31; 2:1-3).

Why is any of that of any importance?

Well, the renewing (the "re-creation"), shows that God can fix what the devil can destroy. Scriptures show that God has a plan to do that in the future (e.g. Act 3:19-21; Isaiah 35:1-2).

Yet further consider that the Bible teaches that Lucifer was "the seal of perfection, full of wisdom and perfect in beauty" (Ezekiel 28:12).

As an angelic being, Lucifer did not need physical sustenance.

Lucifer had it all.

Yet, he sinned (as did certain other angels per 2 Peter 2:4) and pulled a third of the angels with him to the earth (Revelation 12:4) (angels are to be later judged by God's people per 1 Corinthians 6:3).

Lucifer and his rebellion showed that even beings that "had it all" can rebel to try to make things worse. And later, he persuaded the first humans who "had it all" to rebel against God as well (Genesis 3:1-6).

Hence, this helps show that if God gave humans everything they need, so that there would be no poverty, that without godly character, people would still cause problems for themselves and others.

Why Does God Allow Satan to Deceive?

Did Satan's rebellion thwart God's plan?

No.

But doesn't the Bible show that Satan, the "prince of the power of the air" (Ephesians 2:2), broadcasts his selfish and disobedient message? Has the Devil not "blinded" the minds of most of humanity as "the god of this age" (2 Corinthian 4:4)?

Yes and yes.

Doesn't the Bible teach that Satan the Devil "deceives the whole world" (Revelation 12:9)?

Yes.

Well then, why did God allow Satan and his demons to come to deceive people and cause other problems on the earth?

There are a couple of reasons.

The Apostle Paul called our time "this present evil age" (Galatians 1:4), which implies a better age to come.

Why, though, is Satan allowed to have any of his power during our age since he previously rejected God?

Satan's influence helps us learn lessons, and often build character, faster than if it were not present. Faster, so we can overcome and build righteous character through resisting as well as quickly see the fruits of going the wrong way. Each time you resist sin you get spiritually stronger.

Though difficult at times, this acceleration results in less overall suffering.

Let's consider a few things that help illustrate this.

Consider carbon, like a piece of coal. It can break apart relatively easily, but once It is under extreme pressure it can turn into a diamond—which is among the hardest of natural substances. So, the weak becomes strong through pressure. The Bible teaches that Christians, though weak in the world (1 Corinthians 1:26-29), are to be pure like refined gold, silver, or precious stones per 1 Corinthians 3:12.

Next, imagine you want to overcome some heavy object you cannot lift. You could look at the heavy object, but that won't move it. You could bend your arms twenty minutes or so per day and that might make your arms a little stronger—but not too much—or maybe it would take years and years to make any difference.

Or you could work out with heavy weights that you could handle. Lifting them would be harder than simply lifting your arms.

However, lifting weights would not only make your arms stronger than simply bending them, this type of exercise would also make the time necessary to get your arms strong enough to overcome the object much shorter.

Now consider that:

> In 1962, Victor and Mildred Goertzel published a revealing study of 413 "famous and exceptionally gifted people" called Cradles of Eminence. They spent years attempting to understand what produced such greatness, what common thread might run through all of these outstanding people's lives.
>
> Surprisingly, the most outstanding fact was that virtually all of them, 392, had to overcome very difficult obstacles in order to become who they were. (Holy Sweat, Tim Hansel, 1987, Word Books Publisher, p. 134)

What do these examples have to do with why there is a devil?

Allowing the devil to try to tempt humankind essentially speeds up the process of being able to overcome our own flaws and develop righteous character with God's help (Philippians 4:13; James 4:7). The end result of which is that people will be able to overcome faster and with the least suffering possible (cf. Lamentations 3:33; 1 Peter 4:12-13; 3 John 2).

And if God is calling you in this age, He will not allow you to be tempted by Satan or various lusts beyond what you are able to handle (1 Corinthians 10:13).

Resisting Satan and various temptations makes you spiritually stronger (James 1:12, 4:7) and will help you be able to help others in the future (cf. 1 John 4:21). Satan does not want you to believe the truth of the word of God.

Mystery of Truth

The *Cambridge Dictionary* defines 'the truth' as follows:

> **the truth** the real facts about a situation, event, or person:

The truth is something that is genuinely accurate. Yet, philosophers, common people, and leaders have long wondered about the truth.

So, let's notice how the *Cambridge Dictionary* defines 'formal' truth:

> a fact or principle that is thought to be true by most people:

But the above is most certainly not always true. And many have long realized that. Yet, many consider "formal" truth reality and do not accept absolutes like real truth. But beliefs, individual or collective, of themselves are often not true. The Bible warns against those who take counsel of humans instead, truly, of God (Isaiah 30:1; 65:12b). Sin is a factor (cf. Isaiah 59:2a).

When speaking with Jesus, the Roman Prefect Pontius Pilate asked about truth:

[37] Pilate therefore said to Him, "Are You a king then?"

Jesus answered, "You say rightly that I am a king. For this cause I was born, and for this cause I have come into the world, that I should bear witness to the truth. Everyone who is of the truth hears My voice."

[38] Pilate said to Him, "What is truth?" And when he had said this, he went out again to the Jews, and said to them, "I find no fault in Him at all." (John 18:37-38)

Pilate had apparently heard many arguments about truth and concluded that no one could properly define it.

While Jesus did not then answer Pilate's last question, it looks like Pilate went out not expecting an answer. But Jesus said that those of the truth would hear Him.

Shortly before meeting Pilate, John recorded that Jesus did say what the truth was:

[17] Sanctify them by Your truth. Your word is truth. (John 17:17)

The Bible, also, teaches that God cannot lie (Hebrews 6:18, Titus 1:2).

Therefore, it can be concluded that whatever God says is the truth.

Now, this will be considered as circular reasoning, especially to those that do accept the Bible as true. However, once you prove that there is a God and that His word is true (and we have books, such as *Is God's Existence Logical* and *Proof Jesus is the Messiah* that do that), then it is logical to conclude that the word of God is the standard to evaluate what is true.

A lie is something that is opposed to the truth. Therefore, something in conflict with the original inspired word of God is not true, no matter how many people claim to believe it.

Many believe that they should "let their conscience be their guide." But without God's Spirit, the carnal mind cannot discern the truth as it should (1 Corinthians 2:14) as the heart can be desperately wicked (Jeremiah 17:9).

Consider also that Jesus said:

> 4 ... "It is written, 'Man shall not live by bread alone, but by every word that proceeds from the mouth of God.'" (Matthew 4:4)

Humans produce bread from things God created. But the real way to live is by following the word of God.

The Apostle Paul wrote:

> 13 For this reason we also thank God without ceasing, because when you received the word of God which you heard from us, you welcomed it not as the word of men, but as it is in truth, the word of God, which also effectively works in you who believe. 14. For you, brethren, became imitators of the churches of God which are in Judea in Christ Jesus. (1 Thessalonians 2:13-14a).

> 7 ... the word of truth, (2 Corinthians 6:7)

> 13 In Him you also trusted, after you heard the word of truth, the gospel of your salvation; (Ephesians 1:13)

> 5 ...the hope which is laid up for you in heaven, of which you heard before in the word of the truth of the gospel, (Colossians 1:5)

The truth is a mystery to most, because most do not fully trust the true word of God (cf. Colossians 1:5,-6,25-27; 1 Thessalonians 2:13) nor understand much of the good news of the gospel of salvation. Most trust in other humans, who themselves have been deceived by Satan (Revelation 12:9). Jesus stated:

> 8 "These people draw near to Me with their mouth, And honor Me with their lips, But their heart is far from Me. 9 And in vain

they worship Me, Teaching as doctrines the commandments of men. (Matthew 15:8-9)

Trusting more in other humans than God's word leads to vain worship and leads people away from the truth.

Yet, the truth can be known.

The Apostle John wrote:

> [31] Then Jesus said to those Jews who believed Him, "If you abide in My word, you are My disciples indeed. [32] And you shall know the truth, and the truth shall make you free." (John 8:31-32)

> [46] ...And if I tell the truth, why do you not believe Me? [47] He who is of God hears God's words; therefore you do not hear, because you are not of God. (John 8:46-47)

> [37] ...I have come into the world, that I should bear witness to the truth. Everyone who is of the truth hears My voice (John 18:37).

> [6] If we say that we have fellowship with Him, and walk in darkness, we lie and do not practice the truth. [7] But if we walk in the light as He is in the light, we have fellowship with one another, and the blood of Jesus Christ His Son cleanses us from all sin. (1 John 1:6-7)

> [4] He who says, "I know Him," and does not keep His commandments, is a liar, and the truth is not in him. [5] But whoever keeps His word, truly the love of God is perfected in him. By this we know that we are in Him. [6] He who says he abides in Him ought himself also to walk just as He walked. (1 John 2:4-6)

> [18] My little children, let us not love in word or in tongue, but in deed and in truth. [19] And by this we know that we are of the truth, and shall assure our hearts before Him. (1 John 3:18-19)

³ For I rejoiced greatly when brethren came and testified of the truth that is in you, just as you walk in the truth. ⁴ I have no greater joy than to hear that my children walk in truth. (3 John 3-4)

Despite what the Bible says, the connection between the truth being the word of God and being better understood by those that obey God is a mystery to many.

John also penned the following:

3 ... Just and true are Your ways, O King of the saints! (Revelation 15:3)

Walking in God's ways helps us better understand the truth as we live by the truth.

As Christians, sanctified by the word of God (John 17:17), we are to be "rightly dividing the word of truth" (2 Timothy 2:15), while avoiding "worldly and empty chatter, for it will lead to further ungodliness" (2 Timothy 2:16, NASB). Hence, we avoid compromises with the religions of the world.

But what if science contradicts the Bible, like many pundits claim?

Well, "let God be true but every man a liar" (Romans 3:4). Believe the word of God.

Even back in New Testament times, there were those who called error 'science.' Notice:

²⁰ O Timothy, keep that which is committed to thy trust, avoiding profane and vain babblings, and oppositions of science falsely so called:

²¹ Which some professing have erred concerning the faith. (1 Timothy 6:20-21, KJV)

So, there have been those who claimed Christ who have been misled by intellectual leaders who were opposed to the truth.

The Apostle John was inspired to write:

> [26] These things I have written to you concerning those who try to deceive you. (1 John 2:26)

Various scientists have been deceptive and/or have thought that they had facts that disagreed with the word of God. Do not fall for their misinformation.

There is a God (for details, check out the free book, online at ccog.org titled: *Is God's Existence Logical?)* and His word can be relied on for the truth. The Bible warns that "[c]ursed is the man that trusts in man" (Jeremiah 17:5).

The Apostle Paul wrote the following to Timothy about some who were:

> [7] always learning and never able to come to the knowledge of the truth. [8] Now as Jannes and Jambres resisted Moses, so do these also resist the truth: men of corrupt minds, disapproved concerning the faith; [9] but **they will progress no further, for their folly will be manifest to all**, (2 Timothy 3:7-9)

Many claim to be ever learning and interested in the truth, yet most resist the actual truth.

Truth was prophesied to be a scarcer commodity in the end times:

> [12] Yes, and all who desire to live godly in Christ Jesus will suffer persecution. [13] But evil men and impostors will grow worse and worse, deceiving and being deceived. [14] But you must continue in the things which you have learned and been assured of, knowing from whom you have learned *them*, (2 Timothy 3:12-14)

If you will have enough of the "love of the truth" (2 Thessalonians 2:10), and will act on it, you can be spared from a coming massive deceit (2 Thessalonians 2:7-12), and be spared from a dreadful "hour of trial" that is coming to the whole earth (Revelation 3:7-10).

Mystery of Rest

While it would not seem that rest would be a mystery, it has turned out to be so for many.

The Bible shows that God blessed the seventh day (Genesis 2:2-3). The Bible does not teach that God blessed any other day of human choosing. People are "to obey God rather than men" (Acts 5:29).

God provided a weekly physical break for humans. And He makes provisions so humans can keep it (cf. Exodus 16:5; Leviticus 25:18-22).

Many are surprised to realize that they, in the long run, can get more done by working six days instead of seven. But that is true.

And because people do not understand the scriptures, this is a mystery to most.

God inspired the prophet Ezekiel to write:

> [26] Her priests have violated My law and profaned My holy things; they have not distinguished between the holy and unholy, nor have they made known the difference between the unclean and the clean; and they have hidden their eyes from My Sabbaths, so that I am profaned among them. (Ezekiel 22:26)

Many religious leaders violate God's law and they have hidden their eyes related to the Sabbaths. *My Sabbaths* is a reference to the weekly Sabbath as well as the annual Sabbaths that are also known as God's Holy Days. The Sabbaths are a time of physical rest/restoration and spiritual rejuvenation.

The seven day week pictures that just like God gave humans six days to do their work and to rest on the seventh, that God gave humanity six 'one thousand year days' (cf. Psalm 90:4; 2 Peter 3:8) to do humanity's work, but then to live in the 'seventh one thousand year day' in the millennial kingdom (cf. Revelation 20:4-6).

The 6,000/7,000 year plan aligns well with New Testament teachings about being in the "last days" (Acts 2:14-17) which started no later than when Jesus was finishing His earthly ministry (Hebrews 1:1-2). The last two days of the six-thousand years would be the last days of that type of week.

Jewish tradition teaches that this 6,000 year idea was first taught in the school of Elijah the prophet (Babylonian Talmud: Sanhedrin 97a).

In the late second and earlier third centuries, Greco-Roman saints and bishops like Irenaeus (Irenaeus. Adversus haereses, Book V, Chapter 28:2-3; 29:2) and Hippolytus (Hippolytus. On the HexaËmeron, Or Six Days' Work) also understood and taught the 6,000-7,000 years as well as reported that the weekly Sabbath pictured the millennial rest (the seventh of the thousand years).

But after the 4th century rise of Emperor Constantine, many others stopped teaching this.

Despite Greco-Roman Catholics not officially teaching this anymore, God has allowed the Devil and humanity during this 6,000 year age to choose to go the wrong way in order to minimize total suffering and to be part of the process to perfect all humans who will listen to Him— either in this age or the age to come.

Why 6,000 years?

It would seem that God concluded that this would be enough time for humans to try many different ways of life that they thought was best— and multiple generations since Adam and Eve have had that opportunity. So, for thousands of years humans would later be able to better see that the statements in Proverbs 14:12 and 16:25, "There is a way that seems right to a man, But its end is the way of death," are correct.

God knew that this world will get so bad towards the end of those 6,000 years, that "unless those days were shortened, no flesh would be saved" (Matthew 24:22).

After the 6,000 years, Jesus will return, the saints will be resurrected, life on the planet will be saved, and the millennial portion of the Kingdom of God will be established (cf. Revelation 20:4-6)

And this has seemingly been a mystery to most.

Notice something Isaiah was inspired to write:

> [11] For with stammering lips and another tongue He will speak to this people, [12] To whom He said, "This is the rest with which You may cause the weary to rest," And, "This is the refreshing"; Yet they would not hear. (Isaiah 28:11-12)

God promises rest, but because of "stammering lips and another tongue"—wrong teachings and translation issues—most do not accept the refreshing rest that God has provided for each week.

In the New Testament book of Hebrews, two different Greek words are used and often translated into English as "rest." Transliterated into English, they are *katapausis* and *sabbatismos*. Because many translators have erroneously translated both of those words the same, many have been confused. Sabbatismos is used in Hebrews 4:9, whereas katapausis is used in places like Hebrews 4:3.

Because of the future "rest" (katapausis)--the Kingdom of God--spiritual Israel is to enter into (Hebrews 4:3), there remains for them a sabbatismos—a keeping of the Sabbath day now (Hebrews 4:9). This means that Christians will enter the future 'rest' of God's Kingdom even as they now keep the weekly Sabbath rest which looks forward to it. In this age, God's people are to diligently rest the same day as God did (Hebrews 4:9-11a), "lest anyone fall according to the same example of disobedience" (Hebrews 4:11b).

Due to mistranslations and the 'hiding of eyes' by religious teachers regarding God's Sabbaths, biblical rest is still a mystery to many.

Mystery of Sin

Many people seem to be confused about what sin is.

Many act like they can define it.

Yet, it is God, and not humans, who defines sin.

What is sin?

Here is how the Bible defines it:

> [4] Whoever commits sin also commits lawlessness, and sin is lawlessness. (1 John 3:4, NKJV)

> [4] Whosoever committeth sin commmitteth also iniquity; and sin is iniquity. (1 John 3:4, DRB)

> [4] Everyone who sins breaks the law and in fact, sin is lawlessness. (EOB New Testament)

> [4] Whosoever committeth sin transgresseth also the law: for sin is the transgression of the law. (1 John 3:4, KJV)

What law?

God's law, which is in His word (cf. Psalm 119:11), and that includes the Ten Commandments (cf. 1 John 2:3-4; Psalm 119:172; see also the free book, available online at www.ccog.org, titled: *The Ten Commandments: The Decalogue, Christianity, and the Beast*).

Although no one has been forced to sin, the Bible teaches that all have sinned (Romans 3:23).

Why do humans sin?

Well, for the same reason that Eve and Adam sinned. They were deceived by Satan and/or their lusts.

Satan has deceived the whole world (Revelation 12:9). He has used every evil thought he could to influence and deceive all of humankind. Satan has broadcast his philosophy far and wide (cf. Ephesians 2:2) — appealing to vanity, lust and greed to influence us.

Notice the following from the late evangelist Leroy Neff:

> Each of us has been tuned into this deceitful bombardment from an early age. Satan has used this method to insert wrong thoughts, and he uses the environment and circumstances to influence us to make wrong decisions just like Adam and Eve did.
>
> When we were born, we had no hatred or animosity against God or His perfect way. We didn't even know that God existed, or that He had a right way for us to live. But in due time we, too, developed the same attitude as Satan, of selfishness, of greed and lust, and of wanting our own way.
>
> When we were little children, we may have been like those that Christ spoke of (Matthew 18:3, 4). They were humble and teachable — not yet fully deceived by Satan and his society. ...
>
> All human woe, unhappiness, pain and misery have come as a direct result of sin — the violation of God's spiritual and physical laws. Happiness and a full abundant life are the automatic results of obedience to God's Law. (Neff L. All About Sin. Tomorrow's World Magazine. April 1972)

And while Jesus died for all our sins, sin has a cost. And the long-term cost is that it negatively impacts the sinner and one's potential to do even more good. So, do not think that sinning now is good for you (or others), but hopefully all will learn lessons from their sins (cf. 2 Peter 2:18-20), confess them (1 John 1:9), and repent of them (cf. Act 2:37-38).

Because of improper teachings and traditions, many do not recognize sin in this age.

The Apostle Paul wrote:

> [7] For the mystery of lawlessness is working already; there is only the one at present restraining it, until he might be gone out of the midst. [8] And then the lawless one will be revealed, whom the Lord Jesus will consume with the breath of His mouth and will annul by the appearing of His coming, [9] whose coming is according to the working of Satan, in every power, and in signs, and in wonders of falsehood, [10] and in every deception of wickedness unto those perishing, in return for which they did not receive the love of the truth in order for them to be saved. [11] And because of this, God will send to them a working of delusion, for them to believe what is false, [12] in order that all those not having believed the truth but having delighted in unrighteousness should be judged. (2 Thessalonians 2:7-12, Berean Literal Bible)

Part of the "mystery of lawlessness" ("mystery of iniquity" DRB) is that many have not been taught that truth about sin and/or have been taught to reason around God's laws like the Pharisees of Jesus' time and instead accept improper traditions (cf. Matthew 15:1-9). Those without sufficient love of the truth will be cruelly deceived as we get closer to the end of this age.

The Bible teaches, "Do not be deceived, my beloved brethren" (James 1:16).

Yet, we humans tend to deceive ourselves (particularly with Satan's influence) and not realize the extent of our tendencies to stray.

The Apostle James explained the following about temptation and sin:

> [12] Blessed is the man who endures temptation; for when he has been approved, he will receive the crown of life which the Lord has promised to those who love Him. [13] Let no one say when he is tempted, "I am tempted by God"; for God cannot be tempted by evil, nor does He Himself tempt anyone. [14] But each one is tempted when he is drawn away by his own desires and enticed.

15 Then, when desire has conceived, it gives birth to sin; and sin, when it is full-grown, brings forth death. (James 1:12-15)

In order to resist temptation, to get a wrong thought out of your mind that enters it, fill your mind with good thoughts (Philippians 4:8) and turn to God.

What better thoughts are there than those about God and His Word? If you properly resist Satan, the Bible says he will flee (James 4:7).

Resisting makes you spiritually stronger, while indulging in sin makes you weaker.

Sin helps show, for those who are willing to believe, that we need God and His ways.

God understood about the influence of Satan's deception, as well as human lusts, and developed a plan of salvation that takes that into account (for more details on that, please check out the free online book: *Universal OFFER of Salvation. Apokatastasis: Can God save the lost in an age to come? Hundreds of scriptures reveal God's plan of salvation*).

3. What Do the World's Religions Believe?

Various faiths have their beliefs about what the purposes are for the creation. So, let's look at some statements from those that hold to various Eastern and Western religions.

But first, let us consider atheists. Atheist do not believe that humans have any purpose, except perhaps enjoyment or some form of personal fulfillment.

There are some (who may or may not consider themselves as atheists) that believe it would be better If less humans existed:

> Anti-natalism is the belief that human life is objectively worthless and pointless. As The Guardian explains, anti-natalists contend that human reproduction causes unjustified harm to human society (which shouldn't exist to begin with, by this way of thinking) and the planet. Furthermore, parents are guilty of a moral crime by imposing existence on children who have not consented to their existence. ...
>
> anti-natalists often claim that their belief in the worthlessness of human life is motivated by compassion for human life ...
>
> anti-natalists wish to protect humanity from harm by ensuring its obliteration ... (Walsh M. Growing 'Anti-Natalist' Movement Calls For The Extinction Of Humanity... Daily Wire, November 15, 2019)

Basically, anti-natalists believe humans cause more harm than good, life is hard, and thus people should not bring more human beings into the world as doing so will increase total suffering and pain.

But, they are in error about human worth.

Humans do have value. And while there are sufferings, humans were made to contribute and help. There is a meaning to life.

Now, let's see what Hinduism says about humankind's purpose.

Reportedly there are slightly more than one billion Hindus. Here is information about that faith's beliefs:

> According to Hinduism, the meaning (purpose) of life is four-fold: to achieve Dharma, Artha, Kama, and Moksha. The first, dharma, means to act virtuously and righteously. ... The second meaning of life according to Hinduism is Artha, which refers to the pursuit of wealth and prosperity in one's life. ... The third purpose of a Hindu's life is to seek Kama. In simple terms, Kama can be defined as obtaining enjoyment from life. The fourth and final meaning of life according to Hinduism is Moksha, enlightenment. By far the most difficult meaning of life to achieve, Moksha may take an individual just one lifetime to accomplish (rarely) or it may take several. However, it is considered the most important meaning of life and offers such rewards as liberation from reincarnation, self-realization, enlightenment, or unity with God. (Sivakumar A. The Meaning of Life According to Hinduism, October 12, 2014)

So, essentially Hinduism teaches to strive to live righteously, seek prosperity, enjoy life, and attain enlightenment, which according to a Hindu I heard speak, also includes deification. While those Hindu beliefs can be consistent with the Bible, they do not explain why there should be life in the first place.

Reportedly there are slightly more than a half billion Buddhists. Buddhism takes a different view than Hinduism:

> Buddhism denies that there is any permanent and absolute significance of life, and described life as unsatisfactory (s. dukkha) and void (s. sunyata). However, Buddha acknowledged that there is a relative significance of life, and it is through this relative and conditioned nature of life that we can achieve and realize the universal truth. According to the discourses of the Buddha, our lives, and the world, are nothing but phenomena that rise and fall. It is a process of forming and degenerating. (What is the Significance of Life? Buddhanet.net, retrieved 03/21/19)

While Hinduism has many gods, Buddhism does not have one. And, if there is no God, then the Buddhists (like other atheists) are right that life has no absolute significance.

But if there is a divine Spirit Being, and yes it is logical to conclude that there is (to have information that proves so, see also our free booklet, online at ccog.org, *Is God's Existence Logical?*), then it would make more sense that a divine Creator had a real and significant purpose.

Now, both Buddhism and Hinduism teach an idea called Karma. Here is some information from a Buddhist source:

> Karma is the law of moral causation. The theory of Karma is a fundamental doctrine in Buddhism. ... In this world nothing happens to a person that he does not for some reason or other deserve. ... The Pali term Karma literally means action or doing. Any kind of intentional action whether mental, verbal, or physical, is regarded as Karma. It covers all that is included in the phrase "thought, word and deed". Generally speaking, all good and bad action constitutes Karma. In its ultimate sense Karma means all moral and immoral volition. (Sayadaw M. The Theory of Karma. Buddhanet.net, retrieved 07/22/19)

While the Bible does not use the term "Karma" it does teach that one will reap what one sows (Galatians 6:7-8). But unlike Buddhism, the Bible teaches that God directs things (Proverbs 16:9) so ultimately it will work out well for those that accept His will (cf. Romans 8:28). And there will be no end to the increase of peace (Isaiah 9:7).

Now, however, it should be pointed out that Hinduism and Buddhism want the world to be a better place. But they do not understand how the Bible teaches that will happen.

Unlike Buddhists, Muslims believe in a divine Creator who has a purpose for humans. There are reportedly 1.8 billion Muslims. Here is one Islamic view related to why God made people:

> Our body, our spirit, our predisposition to worship God, and our light are gifts sent directly from God to serve as critical means

toward our attaining human perfection. That perfection lies in cultivating those aspects of the spirit that transcend its animating qualities, actualizing our disposition to worship, and refining our light. When this happens, the human is a beautiful creature, and as such, a fitting object of divine love, for as our Prophet mentioned, "Verily, God is beautiful and loves beauty." (Shakir A. The Human in the Qur'an. Journal of the Zaytuna College, June 5, 2018)

Now while Jesus also pointed out that perfection should be the goal (Matthew 5:48), the above does not truly explain why God made humans. However, the following Islamic source gives a reason:

God created man to serve Him, meaning that men should believe in the One God and do good. This is the object of human life. God says, "I have not created men except that they should serve Me." (The Winds That Scatter, 51:56) (What is the purpose of human life in Islam? Muslim Converts Association of Singapore, accessed 03/21/19)

While humans should do good, much of the rest of the above is similar to certain Protestant views as to why God made humans, which we will look at next.

Some Protestant Views

There are different views about why God created humans within the religions already mentioned.

And the same is true among Protestants.

There are reportedly just over 800 million Protestants, and they are divided by many denominations, ministries, and sects (note: the *Continuing* Church of God is NOT Protestant—details as to why are found in our free online books: *The Continuing History of the Church of God* and *Hope of Salvation: How the Continuing Church of God Differs from Protestantism*).

However, despite the variety of Protestants, there seems to be some general agreements on why God made anything.

Notice one Protestant view of why God made humans:

Why Did God Create Humans?

He did so to give himself glory. God created us to live and enjoy relationships as he did. Jesus said, "I have told you this so that my joy may be in you and that your joy may be complete" (John 15:11). ...

To bring glory to God—that is, to exalt him, lift him up, give him praise, to reflect upon him honorable—is in fact our purpose in life. (Bell S. Josh McDowell Ministry. posted April 11, 2016)

We in the CCOG would disagree. God did not create us because He is some ego-driven spiritual entity that needed people to give Him glory. Nor is giving glory to God the purpose of human life. But it is true that God wanted to increase joy.

Here is another, somewhat similar Protestant response:

Why did God create in the first place? Was He bored? Was He lonely? Why did God go through the trouble of making humans?

The Bible tells us that God's ultimate purpose for the universe is to reveal His glory. The Bible tells us that God's ultimate purpose for mankind is to reveal His love. (Was God Bored? All About God Ministries, accessed 03/21/19)

Well, this is slightly closer as love is part of it, but again the implication is that God made everything because of His need to have His ego stroked. God is not vain and does not need that.

Here are views from two other Protestants:

Why Did God Create the World?

The short answer that resounds through the whole Bible like rolling thunder is: *God created the world for his glory*. (Piper J. September 22, 2012. https://www.desiringgod.org/messages/why-did-god-create-the-world accessed 01/16/19)

Why Did God Create?

God did not create because of some limitation within Himself. Instead, He created everything out of nothing in order to put His glory on display for the delight of His created beings and that they might declare His greatness. (Lawson J. Ligonier Ministries, July 3, 2017)

Two more claiming God made things for His personal glory.

So, those Protestant (including Baptist) sources seem to agree. But we in CCOG do not believe they really understand the mystery of God's plan.

Views from the Catholic Church and the Jehovah's Witnesses

What about Roman Catholics?

The *Catechism of the Catholic Church* teaches:

> **293** Scripture and Tradition never cease to teach and celebrate this fundamental truth: "The world was made for the glory of God."[134] St. Bonaventure explains that God created all things "not to increase his glory, but to show it forth and to communicate it",[135] for God has no other reason for creating than his love and goodness: "Creatures came into existence when the key of love opened his hand."[136] The First Vatican Council explains:
>
> This one, true God, of his own goodness and "almighty power", not for increasing his own beatitude, nor for attaining his perfection, but in order to manifest this perfection through the

benefits which he bestows on creatures, with absolute freedom of counsel "and from the beginning of time, made out of nothing both orders of creatures, the spiritual and the corporeal. . ."[137]

294 The glory of God consists in the realization of this manifestation and communication of his goodness, for which the world was created. God made us "to be his sons through Jesus Christ, according to the purpose of his will, *to the praise of his glorious grace*",[138] for "the glory of God is man fully alive; moreover man's life is the vision of God: if God's revelation through creation has already obtained life for all the beings that dwell on earth, how much more will the Word's manifestation of the Father obtain life for those who see God."[139] The ultimate purpose of creation is that God "who is the creator of all things may at last become "all in all", thus simultaneously assuring his own glory and our beatitude.

Now, because of the mention of love, the above is closer than some other sources, though it is not sufficiently complete as it leaves out an important reason.

The late Cardinal John Henry Newman got closer when he wrote the following:

I am created to do something or to be something for which no one else is created. I have a place in God's counsels, in God's world, which no one else has ... If, indeed, I fail, He can raise another, as He could make the stones children of Abraham. Yet I have a part in this great work ... He has not created me for naught. (Newman JH. Meditations and Devotions of the Late Cardinal Newman. Longmans, Green, 1903, p. 301)

The above is basically correct, though it is still not complete. Some Protestants also realize that God will have a work for His saints during eternity, but they tend to be vague about what work or why.

Now, here is what the Jehovah's Witnesses teach in *Lesson 2.3* of its online Bible teachings titled *Why Did God Create Humans?*:

Jehovah created humans to enjoy **life on earth forever** and to know him as their loving Father. (https://www.jw.org/en/bible-teachings/online-lessons/basic-bible-teachings/unit-2/why-did-god-create-man-purpose/#78 accessed 01/16/19)

... why the earth exists? ... It was created to be a beautiful home for humans (https://www.jw.org/en/bible-teachings/online-lessons/basic-bible-teachings/unit-2/why-did-god-create-man-purpose/#85 accessed 01/16/19).

1. God created the earth to be a permanent home for humans
2. God created humans to **live forever** under his loving direction. He will accomplish that purpose (https://www.jw.org /en/bible-teachings/online-lessons/basic-bible-teachings/unit-2/why-did-god-create-man-purpose/#131)

While it is true that God created the earth to be a home for humans, and that God will give those who will properly repent and accept Jesus eternal life, that really does not explain WHY God created humans in the first place.

The Beatific Vision

Some feel that eternity will be spent primarily gazing upon the face of God. This is known as the 'Beatific Vision.'

While the Bible teaches we can see God's face forever (Psalm 41:12), the Beatific Vision is taught by some as the Christian reward and purpose of the creation.

Here is how the *New World Encyclopedia* describes it:

The **Beatific Vision** is a term in Catholic theology describing the direct perception of God enjoyed by those who are in Heaven, imparting supreme happiness or blessedness. In this view, humans' understanding of God while alive is necessarily indirect (mediated), while the Beatific Vision is direct (immediate). ...

Thomas Aquinas explained the Beatific Vision as the ultimate goal of human existence after physical death. Aquinas' formulation of beholding God in Heaven parallels Plato's description of beholding the Good in the world of the Forms, which is not possible while still in the physical body. ...

The philosophy of Plato hints at the concept of the Beatific Vision in the Allegory of the cave, which appears in the Republic Book 7 (514a-520a), speaking through the character of Socrates:

> My opinion is that in the world of knowledge the idea of good (the Good) appears last of all, and is seen only with an effort; and, when seen, is also inferred to be the universal author of all things beautiful and right, parent of light and of the lord of light in this visible world, and the immediate source of reason and truth in the intellectual (517b,c).

For Plato, the Good appears to correspond to God in Christian theology. ...

St. Cyprian of Carthage (third century) wrote of the saved seeing God in the Kingdom of Heaven.

> How great will your glory and happiness be, to be allowed to see God, to be honored with sharing the joy of salvation and eternal light with Christ your Lord and God... to delight in the joy of immortality in the Kingdom of Heaven with the righteous and God's friends. ...

In the thirteenth century, philosopher-theologian Thomas Aquinas, following his teacher Albertus Magnus, described the ultimate goal of a human life as consisting in the intellectual Beatific Vision of God's essence after death. According to Aquinas, the Beatific Vision surpasses both faith and reason. ...

Hindu and Buddhist thought have long spoken of the experience of samadhi, in which the soul finds union with the divine while still in the body. The mystical tradition in Islam speaks of literally seeing with God's eyes: "When I love him, I am his hearing by which he hears; and his sight by which he sees; his hand by which he strikes; and his foot by which he walks" (Hadith of An-Nawawi 38).

George Fox and the other early Quakers believed that direct experience of God was available to all people, without mediation. (Beatific Vision. New World Encyclopedia, 2013. http://www.newworldencyclopedia.org/entry/Beatific_Vision accessed 04/16/19)

The editor of the *Lutheran Journal of Ethics* wrote:

But the end goal of God's purpose for the human creature shines through an eschatological understanding of sanctification, where we are promised the beatific vision of holiness and full communion with God in eternity. (Santos C. Editor's Introduction: Lutherans and Sanctification. © September/October 2017. Journal of Lutheran Ethics, Volume 17, Issue 5)

Many Protestants that believe in the Beatific Vision lean toward the view that this vision is a spiritual, not physical sight (e.g. Ortlund G. Why We Misunderstand the Beatific Vision. First Baptist Church of Ojai, September 26, 2018).

Those who accept versions of the Beatific Vision as the end goal tend to think that seeing God will fill them with His or their own happiness.

Here is an opposing view of that vision from a onetime Church of God writer:

If eternity is to be spent gazing blissfully up into God's face, or having our every wish immediately fulfilled — as many religions teach — after a few months (or after a few octillion years, it doesn't really matter), life would get boring. And once life got boring, it would be sickeningly and fiendishly terrifying. Because there would remain nothing but an unending eternity of boredom to come — with death a wonderful but impossible way of escape (see Luke 20:35-38). This would indeed be the ultimate torture.

But our Eternal Father has a better idea. He has designed a plan in which eternity will not grow progressively more boring. But, as unbelievable as it seems, eternity will grow progressively more exciting, more scintillating, and more enjoyable as each eon follows eon. (Kuhn RL. The God Family - Part Three: To Inhabit Eternity. Good News, July 1974)

Yes, God made what He did so that eternity could be better. Notice something from a deceased Church of God writer:

The God who put this world together did so with a plan in mind. That plan was not the hopeless Nirvana of one major religion of the world which promises you will become an unconscious part of the great whole of nothing with no worries forever — because you have no individual consciousness forever. It is not the bliss of slumbering in a hammock slung between two date palms in an oasis, being fed by voluptuous maidens forever, the promise of which the followers of Allah are assured. It is not walking the golden streets with golden slippers, strumming on a harp with your only worry being how to keep your halo straight, as seems to be the promise of the majority of Protestant groups. It is most certainly not the promise of finally being able to look into the face of God and appreciate the beatific vision (whatever that is), as is the promise to those who follow the Catholic faith: What the God who created everything proposes is to bring you into His very family. To be God as God is God! Not just to be a God in the euphemistic sense of us all being brothers and sisters with God as our figurehead Father, but to share His divine nature completely. ...

God's real plan is practical. He says of His family Kingdom that there will never be an end to its expansion. His plan is to continue adding sons and daughters who look, feel, act like Him and who are composed of the same self-regenerating eternal

49

spirit life as He is, forever! That is why the goal God has set before Himself is a hope that not even He will ever fulfill. Endless, eternal, forever creating an ever-expanding family to enjoy and rule the great creation He has already made — and to have you and me share in future creations without end. A busy, practical, interesting, challenging, ongoing plan that gives an eternal reason to live.

There is no boredom in that plan. Never a time when your interest will run out. No mythical, religious-sounding folderol about some spiritual never-never land where you do nothing forever — but an eternal job of creating, governing! problem-solving with visible benefit. ... He has the power to resurrect you ... (Hill DJ. What the World Needs Now Is...HOPE. Plain Truth, February 1979)

Notice something from a late Church of God leader:

"If a man die, shall he live again?" (Job 14:14). This should be a time of HOPE, because even if THIS WORLD dies — and it shall — there will follow **a RESURRECTION of a new and better world** — a world at PEACE — a world of contentment, happiness, abundance, JOY! God help us to comprehend! Not merely continuous existence — but the full, happy, interesting, ABUNDANT life! Yes — and that for ALL ETERNITY! (Armstrong HW. What Is the Purpose of the Resurrection? Good News, March 1982)

Because many do not fully understand scripture, they have promoted views, like how they teach the beatific vision, which are not fully consistent with God's plan.

Us looking at God does not, of itself, make eternity better. Though Him blessing us forever certainly will do that (cf. Psalm 72:17-19).

All Things Created for Jesus

The New Testament teaches this related to Jesus and the creation:

¹⁵ He is the image of the invisible God, the firstborn over all creation. ¹⁶ For by Him all things were created that are in heaven and that are on earth, visible and invisible, whether thrones or dominions or principalities or powers. All things were created through Him and for Him. Colossians 1:15-16)

² ... His Son, whom He has appointed heir of all things, through whom also He made the worlds; ³ who being the brightness of His glory and the express image of His person, and upholding all things by the word of His power, (Hebrews 1:2-3)

Now, were we simply created to look at Jesus for eternity?

No.

Notice why Jesus said He came:

¹⁰ ... I have come that they may have life, and that they may have *it* more abundantly. (John 10:10)

By have "life" and having it "more abundantly", Jesus is teaching that He came so that we could have a better eternity and that we could help make eternity better.

God did not create humans for the purpose of humans staring at Him for all eternity.

4. Why Does God Allow Suffering?

If Jesus came so that we could have life "more abundantly" (John 10:10), does God allow suffering?

Yes.

Is there a purpose for it?

Yes.

> [31] For the Lord will not cast off forever. [32] Though He causes grief, Yet He will show compassion According to the multitude of His mercies. [33] For He does not afflict willingly, Nor grieve the children of men. (Lamentations 3:31-33)

Notice that God does not willingly afflict nor grieve us. He wants us to do well (cf. 3 John 2).

Seemingly bad things happen to decent people.

Jesus never sinned (Hebrews 4:15), but suffered for us (1 Peter 2:21). And "though He was a Son, yet He learned obedience by the things which He suffered" (Hebrews 5:8).

Why does God allow humans to suffer?

There are a couple of reasons. One is as punishment for/result of our sins to encourage us to not sin and to turn back to God (Lamentations 3:39-40; Leviticus 26:18). And, we should understand that the Bible teaches that God punishes us less than our iniquities deserve (cf. Ezra 9:13; Job 11:6). Now, even people who believe at least those parts of the Bible, realize that.

But there is another, more complicated, reason.

The Apostle Paul tells us that "the creation was subjected to futility, not willingly, but because of Him who subjected it in hope" (Romans 8:20). He also wrote:

¹⁶ Therefore we do not lose heart. Even though our outward man is perishing, yet the inward man is being renewed day by day. ¹⁷ For our light affliction, which is but for a moment, is working for us a far more exceeding and eternal weight of glory, ¹⁸ while we do not look at the things which are seen, but at the things which are not seen. For the things which are seen are temporary, but the things which are not seen are eternal. (2 Corinthians 4:16-18)

People are in the process of being refined—which includes grief and affliction—yet there is hope. Those not called in this age are refined one way (Isaiah 48:10; Jeremiah 9:7), whereas those called are to be refined and purified more like silver and/or gold (Zechariah 13:9; Psalm 66:10; Daniel 11:35, 12:10; 1 Peter 1:7; cf. Revelation 3:18). Hence there are "fiery" trials in this age (1 Peter 1:7; 4:12).

There is a hope for what will be better:

> ⁹ But, beloved, we are confident of better things concerning you, yes, things that accompany salvation, though we speak in this manner. ¹⁰ For God is not unjust to forget your work and labor of love which you have shown toward His name, in that you have ministered to the saints, and do minister. ¹¹ And we desire that each one of you show the same diligence to the full assurance of hope until the end, ¹² that you do not become sluggish, but imitate those who through faith and patience inherit the promises. (Hebrews 6:9-12)

Thus, we are to be patient and confident that God's ways will result in "better things".

Sometimes people suffer for doing good:

> ¹⁷ For *it is* better, if it is the will of God, to suffer for doing good than for doing evil. (1 Peter 3:17)

Note that the above does NOT SAY it is the will of God to inflict suffering on ourselves so that we would be miserable.

Now, the Bible is clear that there are benefits that will arise from the suffering that afflicts us:

> [3] Sorrow is better than laughter, For by a sad countenance the heart is made better. [4] The heart of the wise is in the house of mourning, But the heart of fools is in the house of mirth. (Ecclesiastes 7:3-4)

> [16] The Spirit itself bears witness conjointly with our own spirit, testifying that we are the children of God. [17] Now if we are children, we are also heirs—truly, heirs of God and joint heirs with Christ—if indeed we suffer together with Him, so that we may also be glorified together with Him. (Romans 8:16-17, AFV)

> [18] For I consider that the sufferings of this present time are not worthy *to be compared* with the glory which shall be revealed in us. (Romans 8:18)

> [12] Beloved, do not think it strange concerning the fiery trial which is to try you, as though some strange thing happened to you; [13] but rejoice to the extent that you partake of Christ's sufferings, that when His glory is revealed, you may also be glad with exceeding joy. (1 Peter 4:12-13)

> [11] My son, do not despise the chastening of the Lord, Nor detest His correction; [12] For whom the Lord loves He corrects, Just as a father the son in whom he delights. (Proverbs 3:11-12)

> [5] And you have forgotten the exhortation which speaks to you as to sons: "My son, do not despise the chastening of the Lord, Nor be discouraged when you are rebuked by Him; [6] For whom the Lord loves He chastens, And scourges every son whom He receives."

> [7] If you endure chastening, God deals with you as with sons; for what son is there whom a father does not chasten? [8] But if you are without chastening, of which all have become partakers, then you are illegitimate and not sons. [9] Furthermore, we have had human fathers who corrected us, and we paid them

respect. Shall we not much more readily be in subjection to the Father of spirits and live? [10] For they indeed for a few days chastened us as seemed best to them, but He for our profit, that we may be partakers of His holiness. [11] Now no chastening seems to be joyful for the present, but painful; nevertheless, afterward it yields the peaceable fruit of righteousness to those who have been trained by it. (Hebrews 12:5-11)

Suffering is allowed so that people will be corrected, be trained, build character, and be better from it (see also Romans 5:3-4, 8:17; 2 Thessalonians 1:3-5; James 1:2-4; 2 Peter 1:5-8; Revelation 21:7-8). Trials and problems help build faith, teach humility, teach us lessons, and can help us draw closer to God.

While it can seem overwhelming now, God understands and makes it so His people can bear it (1 Corinthians 10:13). Jesus essentially taught to take it one day at a time (Matthew 6:34). And what He has planned in the future is so beyond what physical sufferings will be in this life (Romans 8:18).

Jesus and God's people have suffered:

[1] Therefore, seeing we also are compassed about with so great a cloud of witnesses, leaving behind all the weight of the sin which surrounds us, let us run with patience the race that is set before us, [2] with our eyes fixed on Jesus, the author and finisher of our faith, who having been offered joy, endured the cross {Gr. stauros – stake}, despising the shame and was seated at the right hand of the throne of God. [3] For consider him that endured such contradiction of sinners against himself lest ye be wearied in your souls and faint. (Hebrews 12:1-3, Jubilee Bible)

Suffering will end:

[12] ... Though I have afflicted you, I will afflict you no more; [13] For now I will break off his yoke from you, And burst your bonds apart. (Nahum 1:12-13)

While this was given as a prophesy related to Nineveh, other scriptures confirm that suffering will end (Revelation 21:4) and the yoke of Satan will be broken (Isaiah 14:12-17; Revelation 20:1-3).

It needs to be pointed out that suffering does not always result from our actions. We, like Jesus, can suffer wrongfully:

> [19] For this *is* commendable, if because of conscience toward God one endures grief, suffering wrongfully. [20] For what credit *is it* if, when you are beaten for your faults, you take it patiently? But when you do good and suffer, if you take it patiently, this *is* commendable before God.

> [21] For to this you were called, because Christ also suffered for us, leaving us an example, that you should follow His steps:

> [22] "Who committed no sin, Nor was deceit found in His mouth";

> [23] who, when He was reviled, did not revile in return; when He suffered, He did not threaten, but committed *Himself* to Him who judges righteously; (1 Peter 2:19-23)

Jesus set an example to us about suffering (1 Peter 2:21-24). As did the prophets (James 5:10-11).

We are to imitate Jesus (1 Peter 2:21-24), as well as the prophet Paul (1 Corinthians 13:2) as he imitated Jesus (1 Corinthians 11:1).

Children

What about children who suffer?

The Bible tells of children who suffer. At least one man was born blind so "that the works of God should be revealed in him" (John 9:3). But the other reason is so that they will build character as well.

What about children who die, are aborted, or killed at an early age?

While those are human tragedies, God has a plan for them—He has not forgotten them (cf. Isaiah 49:15). They, like others uncalled and unchosen in this age, will be part of the second resurrection (Revelation 20:5, 11). And, the Bible says that they will live again—but that time for 100 years per Isaiah 65:20.

Moving Towards Perfection

In the Old Testament, Moses wrote that God's "work is perfect" (Deuteronomy 32:4). In the New Testament, the Apostle James wrote:

> 2 My brethren, count it all joy when you fall into various trials, 3 knowing that the testing of your faith produces patience. 4 But let patience have its perfect work, that you may be perfect and complete, lacking nothing. 5 If any of you lacks wisdom, let him ask of God, who gives to all liberally and without reproach, and it will be given to him. (James 1:2-5)

Suffering looks to be part of moving towards perfection. This DOES NOT mean we are to torture ourselves intentionally like some do, but to patiently endure the trials and sufferings we encounter.

And yes, that is easier to write than to experience—and God knows this (cf. Hebrews 12:11):

> 8 The Lord will perfect *that which* concerns me; (Psalm 138:8)

God is working to perfect YOU!

Consider that the Bible teaches Jesus learned obedience from suffering:

> 8 though He was a Son, yet He learned obedience by the things which He suffered. 9 And having been perfected, He became the author of eternal salvation to all who obey Him, (Hebrews 5:8-9)

His followers should learn that as well.

Jesus taught:

⁴⁸ Therefore you shall be perfect, just as your Father in heaven is perfect. (Matthew 5:48)

Does that mean Christians are now perfect?

No.

The Apostle John clearly taught that true Christians still sin and need forgiveness (1 John 1:8-10).

So, does this mean that Christians should just conclude since this is impossible, that it is okay not to try?

No.

Christians are to overcome with God's help (Romans 12:21; Philippians 4:13; 1 John 4:4) the tests and trials in this life, which helps bring us closer to perfection (James 1:2-4).

The Apostle Paul, while suffering from an affliction, related something Jesus told him:

⁹ And He said to me, "My grace is sufficient for you, for My strength is made perfect in weakness." (2 Corinthians 12:9)

We are being perfected now through what we go through.

It is when Christians are resurrected as God's children that they will be fully perfected (cf. Ephesians 4:13; Hebrews 11:40).

5. Why Did God Make YOU?

What is your purpose?

YOU are not the same as anyone else. The Bible teaches that "all the members do not have the same function ... individually ... God has set the members, each one of them, in the body just as He pleased" (Romans 12:4-5, 1 Corinthians 12:18).

So, you are different. Your destiny is unique and important. Your life has meaning.

What is the biblical meaning of your life?

Who are you?

YOU are one who can give love in a unique way.

And that is something you will be able to do eternally.

In the middle of the last century, the Church of God (Seventh Day) published:

> The Christian lives not only for today; he anticipates a better tomorrow. (What the Church of God Believes. The Bible Advocate and Herald of the Coming Kingdom. October 3, 1949, p. 7)

But a Christian does not simply anticipate a better tomorrow. A true Christian builds character now through the tests, opportunities, and trials in life (cf. Romans 5:1-4) which will help the Christian be able to personally contribute to the "better tomorrow."

Ultimately God has special plans for YOU personally.

God made you to give love in your own individual way (cf. 1 Corinthians 12:20-13:10).

But how?

Essentially, by now living by faith and obedience to God in this life.

By being obedient, making biblical choices, having faith, practicing love, and enduring to the end, Christians will not only build character but make eternity better for themselves and others.

As far as faith goes, since God's existence is a fact (cf. Romans 1:20; see also the free book, available at ccog.org, *Is God's Existence Logical?*), it does not take faith to believe that there is a God. Even the demons believe and tremble (James 2:19). However, it does take faith to trust, believe, and obey God. That is part of the "mystery of faith" (cf. 1 Timothy 3:9; more on faith can be found in the free booklet, available online at ccog.org, *Faith for Those God has Called and Chosen*).

God grants His Holy Spirit to those who "obey Him" (Acts 5:32). That, God's Spirit, is what makes one a real Christian (Romans 8:9-11).

Christians, themselves, later will be changed and perfected at the first resurrection (1 Corinthians 15:50-54; Revelation 20:5-6) in order to help give love and actually make eternity better. This resurrection coincides with the seventh and last trumpet (1 Corinthians 15:52), which is the time part of the mystery of God will be finished (Revelation 10:7).

The Apostle Paul referred to the change itself as "a mystery" (1 Corinthians 15:51).

Those who are currently non-Christian will have this opportunity for change after they are resurrected later (see also the free book, online at ccog.org, *Universal OFFER of Salvation, Apokatastasis: Can God save the lost in an age to come? Hundreds of scriptures reveal God's plan of salvation*).

Do Good

God is good (Mark 10:18; Psalm 143:10) and does what is right (cf. Genesis 18:25).

God also wants us to do good as this pleases Him (Psalm 34:14; Hebrews 13:16).

> [19] You are great in counsel and mighty in work, for your eyes are open to all the ways of the sons of men, to give everyone according to his ways and according to the fruit of his doings. (Jeremiah 32:19)

> [9] And let us not grow weary while doing good, for in due season we shall reap if we do not lose heart. [10] Therefore, as we have opportunity, **let us do good to all**, especially to those who are of the household of faith. (Galatians 6:9-10)

> [5] ... God, [6] who "will render to each one according to his deeds": [7] eternal life to those who by patient continuance in doing good seek for glory, honor, and immortality; (Romans 2:5-7)

God wants good for you and if you truly love and "obey Him" (Acts 5:32; Hebrews 5:9), that is how everything will turn out (Romans 8:28).

Notice the following:

> [24] Nothing *is* better for a man *than* that he should eat and drink, and *that* his soul should enjoy good in his labor. This also, I saw, was from the hand of God. (Ecclesiastes 2:24)

> [12] I know that nothing *is* better for them than to rejoice, and to do good in their lives, [13] and also that every man should eat and drink and enjoy the good of all his labor--it *is* the gift of God. [14] I know that whatever God does, It shall be forever. (Ecclesiastes 3:12-14)

The above is true, essentially because being productive in work is intended to make things better. And humans should enjoy being productive.

Furthermore, God's plan takes into account what has happened to you. Notice Old Testament teachings related to that:

[11] The counsel of the Lord stands forever, The plans of His heart to all generations. [12] Blessed *is* the nation whose God *is* the LORD, The people He has chosen as His own inheritance. [13] The LORD looks from heaven; He sees all the sons of men. [14] From the place of His dwelling **He looks On all the inhabitants of the earth; [15] He fashions their hearts individually; He considers all their works.** (Psalm 33:11-15)

[1] For I considered all this in my heart, so that I could declare it all: that the righteous and the wise and their works *are* in the hand of God. (Ecclesiastes 9:1a)

[9] A man's heart plans his way, But the LORD directs his steps. (Proverbs 16:9)

[24] A man's steps are of the LORD; How then can a man understand his own way? (Proverbs 20:24)

[73] Your hands have made me and fashioned me; (Psalm 119:73)

[17] ... "God shall judge the righteous and the wicked, For *there* is a time there for every purpose and for every work." (Ecclesiastes 3:17)

Notice, now, passages in the New Testament:

[11] But the one and the same Spirit is operating in all these things, dividing separately to each one as *God* Himself desires. ... [27] Now you are *the* body of Christ, and *you are all* individual members. (1 Corinthians 12:11, 27, AFV)

[7] Do not be deceived, God is not mocked; for whatever a man sows, that he will also reap. [8] For he who sows to his flesh will of the flesh reap corruption, but he who sows to the Spirit will of the Spirit reap everlasting life. (Galatians 6:7-8)

[10] For God *is* not unjust to forget your work and labor of love which you have shown toward His name ... (Hebrews 6:10)

God has a plan for ALL! That includes YOU INDIVIDUALLY whether you are called in this age or not. And He considers ALL OF YOUR WORKS.

All that you have been through, all that you have suffered, all of which you accomplished, etc. is preparing YOU to make eternity better (unless you will ultimately refuse to support God's Kingdom). Everything you have been through has been preparing you for the calling and work God has for you! YOU will be able to give in a unique way and help make eternity better!

The Bible mentions that just like the body has parts like hands and eyes and parts for smelling, hearing, and other things (1 Corinthians 12:12-26), we all have our unique part in the eternal plan God has. Yes, your role could be quite different from the other billions of humans—don't think God does not have a real plan for YOU.

Furthermore, you are accountable for what you do (Romans 14:12). God will judge based on what you do (Ecclesiastes 12:14; Revelation 20:12) as well as what you fail to do (Matthew 25:24-30). The more you do what you should do, the more you will make eternity better for your own self and others. The more you do not do what you should not do, you will make eternity better for your own self and others. God is a righteous judge (2 Timothy 4:8).

The Bible teaches that we shall be rewarded according to our works (Matthew 16:27; Romans 2:6; Proverbs 24:12; Jeremiah 17:10; Revelation 22:12)! And we will be able to help more people because of that (cf. Luke 19:15-19). The Bible says that after death, our works follow us (cf. Revelation 14:13)—which basically means that what we learned and developed while physical will shape how we will be able to give and work throughout eternity.

Everything God has done He has had a reason for (Ezekiel 14:23). Including the length of our lives, which is usually a mystery for us (cf. Ecclesiastes 9:12).

"Have faith in God" (Mark 11:22) as He has fantastic reasons for everything He does—even when it does not always seem that way to us (cf. Hebrews 12:11; Romans 8:28).

Many have erroneously judged God based on their own conclusions, yet the Bible also teaches:

> [5] Therefore **judge nothing before the time**, until the Lord comes, who will both bring to light the hidden things of darkness and reveal the counsels of the hearts. Then each one's praise will come from God. (1 Corinthians 4:5)

Some things have been hidden. We also do not know everything about any human.

All people are not the same. God has an individual plan for each of us (1 Corinthians 12:4-12).

God is working with all so that each of us can have our part in eternity! As scripture teaches:

> [17] The work of righteousness will be peace, And the effect of righteousness, quietness and assurance forever. (Isaiah 32:17)

> [11] You will show me the path of life; In Your presence is fullness of joy; At Your right hand are pleasures forevermore. (Psalm 16:11)

Peace and pleasures forevermore. A better eternity!

What is something YOU SHOULD DO?

> [11] Come, you children, listen to me; I will teach you the fear of the Lord. [12] Who is the man who desires life, And loves many days, that he may see good? [13] Keep your tongue from evil, And your lips from speaking deceit. [14] Depart from evil and do good; Seek peace and pursue it. (Psalm 34:11-14)

> [3] Trust in the Lord, and do good; Dwell in the land, and feed on His faithfulness. [4] Delight yourself also in the Lord, And He shall give you the desires of your heart. (Psalm 37:3-4)

DO GOOD! TRUST GOD.

What does all this mean?

It means that God created what He did so His creation could do good.

Or more specifically, God created everything He did so that eternity would be better!

Isn't that great?

> [3] ... Great and marvelous are Your works, Lord God Almighty! (Revelation 15:3)

> [19] Oh, how great is Your goodness, Which You have laid up for those who fear You, Which You have prepared for those who trust in You In the presence of the sons of men! (Psalm 31:19)

God's goodness is great because of what He has prepared for us to come.

In Hebrews 11:4-12, starting with Abel, we learn about various ones called of God in the Old Testament. And referring to them, notice what the verses that follow teach:

> [13] These all died in faith, not having received the promises, but having seen them afar off were assured of them, embraced them and confessed that they were strangers and pilgrims on the earth. [14] For those who say such things declare plainly that they seek a homeland. [15] And truly if they had called to mind that country from which they had come out, they would have had opportunity to return. [16] But now **they desire a better, that is, a heavenly country.** Therefore God is not ashamed to be called their God, **for He has prepared a city for them.** (Hebrews 11:13-16)

So at least since the time of Abel, people have had faith that God had a plan for something better, and that God is the God of those who truly understood that. The "city" is New Jerusalem which will come down to the earth from heaven (Revelation 21:2).

The plan is for things to get better.

Consider the following from the New Testament:

> [17] Therefore, to him who knows to do good and does not do *it*, to him it is sin. (James 4:17)

Doesn't that mean Christians are to do good?

Doing good is making things better.

Early Church Writers on Doing Good and Deification

Early church writers had some understanding and gave clues about the purpose of the mystery of God's plan.

In the second century (A.D.) Polycarp of Smyrna, who was ordained by one or more of the original apostles, wrote:

> Let us be zealous in the pursuit of that which is good (Polycarp's Letter to the Philippians, Chapter 6)

> He {Jesus} teaches ... for the fruit of the eternal reward. (Polycarp, Fragments from Victor of Capua, section 4)

Similarly, Melito of Sardis, who was a later successor to Polycarp, wrote:

> He has given thee a mind endowed with freedom; He has set before thee objects in great number, that thou on thy part mayest distinguish the nature of each thing and choose for thyself that which is good; (Melito. A Discourse Which Was in the Presence of Antoninus Caesar. In Ante-Nicene Fathers by Roberts and Donaldson, Volume 8, 1885. Hendrickson Publishers, Peabody (MA), printing 1999, p. 755)

Learning to do good builds character. When we choose to do what is good we help to make things better.

Melito understood that God gave humans freedom of choice and we are to choose what is good. Despite Adam and Eve choosing to transgress, which in essence brought slavery (cf. Romans 6:16-17), Melito explained:

> But man, who is by nature capable of receiving good and evil as soil of the earth is capable of receiving seeds from both sides, welcomed the hostile and greedy counselor, and by having touched that tree transgressed the command, and disobeyed God. (Melito. The Homily On the Passover by Melito, line 48)

Melito also understood that Jesus was part of the plan to deliver us from the slavery of sin:

> Well, the truth of the matter is the mystery of the Lord is both old and new ... For it was through the voice of prophecy that the mystery of the Lord was proclaimed. ...This is the one who delivered us from slavery into freedom, from darkness into light, from death into life, from tyranny into an eternal kingdom, and who made us a new priesthood, and a special people forever. (Melito. The Homily On the Passover by Melito, lines 58,61,68)

Yes, forever, for eternity. And it was through the mystery of prophecy—prophecies that were not understood as well as they should have been by religious leaders of Jesus' time—Jesus was proclaimed before He came (for hundreds of those prophecies, check out the free book, online at www.ccog.org titled: *Proof Jesus is the Messiah*).

Irenaeus of Lyon claimed to have been taught by Polycarp of Smyrna. Irenaeus wrote that Christians have "the hope of the resurrection to eternity" (Irenaeus. Against Heresies, Book IV, Chapter 18, para 5). And yes, resurrected Christians will live throughout eternity.

The Psalms teach:

> [20] You, who have shown me great and severe troubles, Shall revive me again, And bring me up again from the depths of the

earth. 21 You shall increase my greatness, And comfort me on every side. (Psalm 71:20-21)

After the resurrection (also referred to as reviving again) God will increase the greatness of His servants.

How much so?

Jesus cited the "you are Gods" (John 10:34) portion of Psalm 82:6 which is a teaching related to ultimate deification to those who will be willing to live God's way.

Irenaeus also taught that:

> ... there is none other called God by the Scriptures except the Father of all, and the Son, **and those who possess the adoption** (Irenaeus. Adversus haereses, Book IV, Preface, Verse 4)

> "I said, You are all the sons of the Highest, and gods; but you shall die like men." He speaks undoubtedly these words to those who have not received the gift of adoption, but who despise the incarnation of the pure generation of the Word of God, defraud human nature of promotion into God, and prove themselves ungrateful to the Word of God, who became flesh for them. For it was for this end that the Word of God was made man, and He who was the Son of God became the Son of man, that man, having been taken into the Word, and receiving the adoption, might become the son of God. For by no other means could we have attained to incorruptibility and immortality, unless we had been united to incorruptibility and immortality. Irenaeus. Adversus haereses, Book III, Chapter 19, Verse 1).

The Apostle John wrote:

> [2] Beloved, now are we children of God, and what we shall be has not yet been manifested; we know that if it is manifested we shall be like him, for we shall see him as he is. (1 John 3:2, Darby Bible Translation)

Because Jesus has not yet returned, Christians have not yet changed to be like Him—but being so changed is part of the plan (cf. 1 Corinthians 15:50-53). There is still some mystery as far as how we will look (1 Corinthians 13:12), but God's plan involves deification (Romans 8:29; Acts 17:29; Matthew 5:48; Ephesians 3:14-19; Malachi 2:15).

In the early second century, Ignatius of Antioch wrote:

> For it is not my desire to act towards you as a man-pleaser, but as pleasing God, even as also you please Him. For neither shall I ever have such [another] opportunity of attaining to God ... entitled to the honour of a better work ... It is good to set from the world unto God, that I may rise again to Him. ... Suffer me to become food for the wild beasts, through whose instrumentality it will be granted me to attain to God ... I desire the drink of God, namely His blood, which is incorruptible love and eternal life. (Ignatius. Letter to the Romans, Chapters 2,4).

> He is the door of the Father, by which enter in Abraham, and Isaac, and Jacob, and the prophets, and the apostles, and the Church. All these have for their object the attaining to the unity of God (Ignatius. Letter to the Romans, Chapter 9).

So, Ignatius taught that the goal for God's people was deification and to do a better, eternal, work.

Later in the second century, Theophilus of Antioch wrote:

> To those who by patient continuance in well-doing seek immortality, He will give life everlasting, joy, peace, rest, and abundance of good things, which neither has eye seen, nor ear heard, nor has it entered into the heart of man to conceive. (Theophilus. To Autolycus, Book I, Chapter 14)

> Wherefore also, when man had been formed in this world, it is mystically written in Genesis, as if he had been twice placed in Paradise; so that the one was fulfilled when he was placed there, and the second will be fulfilled after the resurrection and judgment. For just as a vessel, when on being fashioned it has

69

some flaw, is remoulded or remade, that it may become new and entire; so also it happens to man by death. For somehow or other he is broken up, that he may rise in the resurrection whole; I mean spotless, and righteous, and immortal. ...

For if He had made him immortal from the beginning, He would have made him God ... so that if he should incline to the things of immortality, keeping the commandment of God, **he should receive as reward from Him immortality, and should become God** ... For God has given us a law and holy commandments; and every one who keeps these can be saved, and, obtaining the resurrection, can inherit incorruption (Theophilus of Antioch. To Autolycus, Book 2, Chapters 26, 27, p. 105).

he who acts righteously shall escape the eternal punishments, and be thought worthy of the eternal life from God. (Theophilus. To Autolycus, Book II, Chapter 34)

But those who worship the eternal God, They shall inherit everlasting life, (Theophilus. To Autolycus, Book II, Chapter 36)

And we have learned a holy law; but we have as lawgiver Him who is really God, who teaches us to act righteously, and to be pious, and to do good. (Theophilus. To Autolycus, Book III, Chapter 9)

So, Theophilus taught deification and doing good for those who were real Christians.

In the third century, the Catholic saint and Bishop Hippolytus of Rome wrote:

The Father of immortality sent the immortal Son and Word into the world, who came to man in order to wash him with water and the Spirit; and He, begetting us again to incorruption of soul and body, breathed into us the breath (spirit) of life, and endued us with an incorruptible panoply. If, therefore, man has become immortal, he will also be God. And if he is made God by water and the Holy Spirit after the regeneration of the layer he is found to be also joint-heir with Christ after the resurrection from the dead (Hippolytus. The Discourse on the Holy Theophany, Chapter 8).

> For, by progressing in virtue, and attaining to better things, "reaching forth to those things which are before," {Philippians 3:13, KJV} according to the word of the blessed Paul, we rise ever to the higher beauty. I mean, however, of course, spiritual beauty, so that to us too it may be said hereafter, "The King greatly desired your beauty." (Hippolytus. Fragments from the Scriptural Commentaries of Hippolytus)

Thus, Hippolytus taught deification and that Christians, by progressing in virtue, attain better things.

In the 4th century, the Greco-Roman saint and Bishop Ambrose of Milan taught:

> Then a Virgin conceived, and the Word became flesh that flesh might become God (Ambrose of Milan. Concerning Virginity (Book I, Chapter 11).

In the 4th century, the Greco-Orthodox saint and Bishop John Chrysostom wrote:

> ... the man can become God, and a child of God. For we read, "I have said, You are gods, and all of you are children of the Most High" (John Chrysostom. Homily 32 on the Acts of the Apostles).

Deification was understood to be a goal for humans since at least the time of Jesus.

Work to Do Good

Solomon wrote that people are to consider the work of God (Ecclesiastes 7:13). Many people do not understand the work of God or consider it well enough--but they should (cf. Matthew 6:33). There is a work to be done now to support (Matthew 24:14, 28:19-20; Romans

9:28; 2 Corinthians 9:6-8; Revelation 3:7-10). And that is good to do (cf. 2 Corinthians 9:6-14; Revelation 3:7-13).

Over two dozen times (NKJV) the Bible specifically says to "do good." We do good by working to help others. We do good by loving God and our neighbors (Matthew 22:37-39)—other humans.

Christians are to support the work of God to reach others (Matthew 24:14, 28:19-20; Romans 10:15, 15:26-27).

The purpose of work is to make things better:

> [5] The plans of the diligent lead surely to plenty, (Proverbs 21:5a)

> [23] In all labor there is profit, (Proverbs 14:23)

> [23] In all labour there is advantage (Proverbs 14:23, Young's Literal Translation)

Working should provide a benefit (advantage) to all.

The Apostle Paul wrote:

> [12] Therefore, my beloved, as you have always obeyed, not as in my presence only, but now much more in my absence, work out your own salvation with fear and trembling; [13] for it is God who works in you both to will and to do for His good pleasure. (Philippians 2:12-13)

We are to work for God's good pleasure—which is to increase love and make eternity better.

God has a job for each of us:

> [15] You shall call, and I will answer You; You shall desire the work of Your hands. (Job 14:15)

YOU, too, are the work of God's hands! He has a plan for you and it involves you doing a work to help make eternity better.

Writer Maria Popova made the following observation:

> The mystery of what makes you and your childhood self the same person despite a lifetime of changes is, after all, one of the most interesting questions of philosophy. (Popova M. Grace Paley on the Art of Growing Older. Brain Pickings, September 3, 2015)

While that is a mystery to many, it is not a mystery to God. God is working with all of us to help us be the best that we can be. As well as to assist others.

Consider that the reason to invent things is usually to make things better.

The reason God "invented" humans was to make eternity better.

Paul and Barnabas stated:

> [18] Known to God from eternity are all His works. (Acts 15:18)

God created people and placed them on this earth as part of His plan for good work:

> [8] For by grace you have been saved through faith, and that not of yourselves; it is the gift of God, [9] not of works, lest anyone should boast. [10] For we are His workmanship, created in Christ Jesus for good works, which God prepared beforehand that we should walk in them. (Ephesians 2:8-10)

All humans?

All who accept God's plan will make eternity better. And that will be all who ever lived except the incorrigibly wicked (for more details on that, check our free online book: *Universal OFFER of Salvation, Apokatastasis: Can God save the lost in an age to come? Hundreds of scriptures reveal God's plan of salvation*).

Jesus declared that there was a place for each of us:

¹ "Do not let your hearts be troubled. You believe in God; believe in Me as well. ² In My Father's house are many rooms. If it were not so, would I have told you that I am going away to prepare a place for you? ³ And if I go and prepare a place for you, I will come back and welcome you into My presence, so that you also may be where I am. (John 14:1-3, BSB)

A place for YOU means that Jesus is promising a place that will be best for you. For your abilities. Do not worry that you cannot be a happy and contributing member of the Kingdom of God. God is faithful to finish the work He has begun in you (cf. Philippians 1:6).

God's plan for human beings shall last forever:

¹⁴ I know that whatever God does, It shall be forever. (Ecclesiastes 3:14)

The Bible shows that Jesus, Himself, came to make things better:

⁶ ... He is also Mediator of a better covenant, which was established on better promises. (Hebrews 8:6)

Christians have a hope for the better—and this should be comforting:

¹⁹ ... there is the bringing in of a better hope, through which we draw near to God. (Hebrews 7:19)

¹³ But I do not want you to be ignorant, brethren, concerning those who have fallen asleep, lest you sorrow as others who have no hope. ¹⁴ For if we believe that Jesus died and rose again, even so God will bring with Him those who sleep in Jesus.

¹⁵ For this we say to you by the word of the Lord, that we who are alive and remain until the coming of the Lord will by no means precede those who are asleep. ¹⁶ For the Lord Himself will descend from heaven with a shout, with the voice of an archangel, and with the trumpet of God. And the dead in Christ will rise first. ¹⁷ Then we who are alive and remain shall be caught up together with them in the clouds to meet the Lord in

the air. And thus we shall always be with the Lord. [18] Therefore comfort one another with these words. (1 Thessalonians 4:13-18)

[34] ... knowing yourselves to have a better and abiding possession. (Hebrews 10:34, Berean Literal Bible)

God created all that He did so that eternity would be better. It will be better forever (cf. Jeremiah 32:38-41).

Making things better for us pleases God, which is also better. And yes, God can be pleased (cf. Hebrews 11:5, 13:16; 1 Peter 2:19-20, NLT)--is that not better for God as well?

God created what He did so eternity would be better.

That is why He created the universe and that is why He created men and women.

God's plan includes all who will heed His call in this age (see also: *Is God Calling You?*) and others in the age to come (see also the free online book: *Universal OFFER of Salvation. Apokatastasis: Can God save the lost in an age to come? Hundreds of scriptures reveal God's plan of salvation*).

Christians need to understand that their individual part is to make eternity better.

But this MUST be done God's way.

[12] There is a way that seems right to a man, But its end is the way of death. (Proverbs 14:12; 16:25)

There are people who think they are making the world better in many ways. And as long as it aligns with God's ways, hopefully they are.

Yet, there are people who think they are making the world better when they protest in favor of abortion rights and various forms of immorality denounced by the Bible.

There are people who think they are making the world better when they promote pagan practices as good.

Sadly, most people persuade themselves and trust in the view of others, older traditions, their desires, and/or their heart over the Bible. Yet, scripture warns:

> [9] "The heart is deceitful above all things, And desperately wicked; Who can know it? [10] I, the Lord, search the heart, I test the mind, Even to give every man according to his ways, According to the fruit of his doings. (Jeremiah 17:9-10)

Do you have a heart willing to do things God's way?

Really? Truly?

Hopefully you do.

While God wants people to do good, those with deceitful hearts are not doing so:

> [20] He who has a deceitful heart finds no good, And he who has a perverse tongue falls into evil. (Proverbs 17:20)

Even when things look difficult from a physical perspective, trust God:

> [9] Oh, fear the Lord, you His saints! There is no want to those who fear Him. [10] The young lions lack and suffer hunger; But those who seek the Lord shall not lack any good thing. (Psalm 34:9-10)

> [31] "Therefore do not worry, saying, 'What shall we eat?' or 'What shall we drink?' or 'What shall we wear?' [32] For after all these things the Gentiles seek. For your heavenly Father knows that you need all these things. [33] But seek first the kingdom of God and His righteousness, and all these things shall be added to you. [34] Therefore do not worry about tomorrow, for tomorrow will worry about its own things. Sufficient for the day is its own trouble. (Matthew 6:31-34)

To maximize your potential for yourself and others, trust God and have Him as your decision-making advisor:

> [5] Trust in the Lord with all your heart, And lean not on your own understanding; [6] In all your ways acknowledge Him, And He shall direct your paths. [7] Do not be wise in your own eyes; Fear the Lord and depart from evil. [8] It will be health to your flesh, And strength to your bones. (Proverbs 3:5-8)

Do not be so wise in your own eyes that you will not fully trust in God.

You will be better off trusting in God.

Work and support God's work to reach others.

6. There is a Long Term Plan

Now God is "the High and Lofty One Who inhabits eternity, whose name is Holy" (Isaiah 57:15).

Christians, as heirs of God now and literal children of God to be glorified with Him in the near future (Romans 8:16-17), will eventually do the same thing. Christians will inhabit eternity (though, unlike God, we all will have had a beginning).

God, Himself, has a long range plan in mind:

> [20] For the creation was subjected to futility, not willingly, but because of Him who subjected it in hope; [21] because the creation itself also will be delivered from the bondage of corruption into the glorious liberty of the children of God. [22] For we know that the whole creation groans and labors with birth pangs together until now. [23] Not only that, but we also who have the firstfruits of the Spirit, even we ourselves groan within ourselves, eagerly waiting for the adoption, the redemption of our body. [24] For we were saved in this hope, but hope that is seen is not hope; for why does one still hope for what he sees? [25] But if we hope for what we do not see, we eagerly wait for it with perseverance. (Romans 8:20-25)

God knew that there would be difficulties within His creation, but He has a plan.

Notice three translations of Jeremiah 29:11:

> [11] For I know the plans I have for you," declares the LORD, "plans to prosper you and not to harm you, plans to give you hope and a future. (Jeremiah 29:11, NIV)

> [11] For I know the thoughts that I think towards you, saith the Lord, thoughts of peace, and not of affliction, to give you an end and patience. (Jeremiah 29:11, Douay-Rheims)

11 For I know the plans I have for you," says the LORD. "They are plans for good and not for disaster, to give you a future and a hope. (Jeremiah 29:11, New Living Translation)

Some quote Jeremiah 29:11 as proof that God has a plan for them. And while God does have a plan for all, many tend to not consider that verse in context.

Notice what the Bible teaches:

11 For I know the thoughts that I think toward you, says the Lord, thoughts of peace and not of evil, to give you a future and a hope. 12 Then you will call upon Me and go and pray to Me, and I will listen to you. 13 And you will seek Me and find Me, when you search for Me with all your heart. 14 I will be found by you, says the Lord, and I will bring you back from your captivity; I will gather you from all the nations and from all the places where I have driven you, says the Lord, and I will bring you to the place from which I cause you to be carried away captive. (Jeremiah 29:11-14)

Notice that the plan was exile. To be a sojourner, to be a pilgrim. So, we believers should not be surprised that we do not always fit in. Consider also what the Apostle Peter wrote:

9 But you are a chosen generation, a royal priesthood, a holy nation, His own special people, that you may proclaim the praises of Him who called you out of darkness into His marvelous light; 10 who once were not a people but are now the people of God, who had not obtained mercy but now have obtained mercy.

11 Beloved, I beg you as sojourners and pilgrims, abstain from fleshly lusts which war against the soul, 12 having your conduct honorable among the Gentiles, that when they speak against you as evildoers, they may, by your good works which they observe, glorify God in the day of visitation. (1 Peter 2:9-12)

17 For the time has come for judgment to begin at the house of God; and if it begins with us first, what will be the end of those who do not obey the gospel of God? 18 Now "If the righteous one is scarcely saved, Where will the ungodly and the sinner appear?" (1 Peter 4:17-18)

28 And we know that all things work together for good to those who love God, to those who are the called according to His purpose. (Romans 8:28)

Sometimes we get confused, but consider scripture teaches:

24 "Teach me, and I will hold my tongue; Cause me to understand wherein I have erred. (Job 6:24)

8 "For My thoughts are not your thoughts, Nor are your ways My ways," says the Lord. 9 "For as the heavens are higher than the earth, So are My ways higher than your ways, And My thoughts than your thoughts. (Isaiah 55:8-9)

Believe and understand that God has a plan and is not making mistakes. Have faith (see also our free online booklet: *Faith for Those God has Called and Chosen*).

You will be better off because of those difficulties if you trust God (Hebrews 12:5-11; Proverbs 3:5-8). And if you were called, chosen, and faithful in this age (Revelation 17:14), you will reign on the earth as kings and priests (Revelation 5:10) with Jesus during the millennial age (Revelation 20:4-6).

Understand that both the Father and Son suffer from sins of humanity (cf. Genesis 6:5-6), plus through the suffering that Jesus undertook to die for our sins (cf. 1 Peter 4:1). Jesus voluntarily put Himself through this (John 10:18), but did so to make eternity better.

There are lessons we need to learn in this life in order to build the type of character that will help us make eternity better.

[1] Therefore, having been justified by faith, we have peace with God through our Lord Jesus Christ, [2] through whom also we have access by faith into this grace in which we stand, and rejoice in hope of the glory of God. [3] And not only that, but we also glory in tribulations, knowing that tribulation produces perseverance; [4] and perseverance, character; and character, hope. (Romans 5:1-4)

[5] But also for this very reason, giving all diligence, add to your faith virtue, to virtue knowledge, [6] to knowledge self-control, to self-control perseverance, to perseverance godliness, [7] to godliness brotherly kindness, and to brotherly kindness love. [8] For if these things are yours and abound, you will be neither barren nor unfruitful in the knowledge of our Lord Jesus Christ. (2 Peter 1:5-8)

You might not think you benefit from difficulties and trials, but if you are a Christian, you should.

Notice something that the late Herbert W. Armstrong wrote:

WHY did the Creator God put MAN on the earth? For God's ultimate supreme purpose of reproducing himself--of recreating himself, as it were, by the supreme objective of creating the righteous divine character ultimately in millions unnumbered begotten and born children who shall become God beings, members of the God family. Man was to improve the physical earth as God gave it to him, finishing its creation (which sinning angels had deliberately refused to do) and, in so doing, to RESTORE the GOVERNMENT OF GOD, with God's WAY of life; and further, in this very process FINISHING THE CREATION OF MAN by the development of God's holy, righteous CHARACTER, with man's own assent. Once this perfect and righteous character is instilled in man, and man converted from mortal flesh to immortal spirit, then is to come the INCREDIBLE HUMAN POTENTIAL--man being BORN INTO the divine FAMILY of God, restoring the government of God to the earth, and then participating in the completion of the CREATION over the entire endless expanse of the UNIVERSE! ... God shall have reproduced

HIMSELF untold millions of times over! So, on the sixth day of that re-creation week, God (Elohim) said, "Let us make man in our image, after our likeness" (Gen. 1:26). Man was made to have (with his assent) a special relationship with his Maker! He was made in the form and shape of God. He was given a spirit (essence in form) to make the relationship possible (Armstrong HW. *Mystery of the Ages*. Dodd Mead, 1985, pp. 102-103).

The purpose of building character is to be better and to be able to serve better.

How do we build character?

Well, the best way is by obeying Him.

And that is for our good.

> [19] I call heaven and earth as witnesses today against you, that I have set before you life and death, blessing and cursing; therefore choose life, that both you and your descendants may live; [20] that you may love the Lord your God, that you may obey His voice, and that you may cling to Him, for He is your life and the length of your days; and that you may dwell in the land which the Lord swore to your fathers, to Abraham, Isaac, and Jacob, to give them." (Deuteronomy 30:19-20)

> [12] "And now, Israel, what does the Lord your God require of you, but to fear the Lord your God, to walk in all His ways and to love Him, to serve the Lord your God with all your heart and with all your soul, [13] and to **keep the commandments of the Lord and His statutes which I command you today for your good**? (Deuteronomy 10:12-13)

Notice that God gave commandments for our good.

You might say that was in the Old Testament, and that love is what is important.

To a degree you would be right.

To a degree?

Yes, to the degree that you are willing to obey God's commandments, which are loving rules for our good, you would be right.

Jesus taught:

> [15] If you love Me, keep My commandments. (John 14:15)

> [9] "As the Father loved Me, I also have loved you; abide in My love. [10] If you keep My commandments, you will abide in My love, just as I have kept My Father's commandments and abide in His love. (John 15:9-10)

God loved us and made us so that we can accept and benefit from that love. Every biblically right choice, right decision, and right action we make helps us build character. This will help us personally as well as others.

The Apostle Paul wrote:

> [1] Imitate me, just as I also imitate Christ. (1 Corinthians 11:1)

> 12 ... the law is not of faith, but "the man who does them shall live by them". (Galatians 3:12)

> [12] ... the commandment holy and just and good. (Romans 7:12)

The Apostle James and Jesus declared that love was tied in with God's commandments:

> [8] If you really fulfill the royal law according to the Scripture, "You shall love your neighbor as yourself," you do well; [9] but if you show partiality, you commit sin, and are convicted by the law as transgressors. [10] For whoever shall keep the whole law, and yet stumble in one point, he is guilty of all. [11] For He who said, "Do not commit adultery," also said, "Do not murder." Now if you do not commit adultery, but you do murder, you have become a transgressor of the law. (James 2:8-11)

[37] Jesus said to him, "'You shall love the Lord your God with all your heart, with all your soul, and with all your mind.' [38] This is the first and great commandment. 39 And the second is like it: 'You shall love your neighbor as yourself.' [40] On these two commandments hang all the Law and the Prophets." (Matthew 22:37-40)

The purpose of the commandments is to show love, make us better, and help others to be better.

[13] Let us hear the conclusion of the whole matter:

Fear God and keep His commandments,
For this is man's all.
[14] For God will bring every work into judgment,
Including every secret thing,
Whether good or evil. (Ecclesiastes 12:13-14)

The Ten Commandments were not some arbitrary rules or burden.

Notice something from the Old and New Testaments:

[18] Where there is no revelation, the people cast off restraint; But happy is he who keeps the law. (Proverbs 29:18)

[3] Dear friends, although I have been eager to write to you about our common salvation, I now feel compelled instead to write to encourage you to contend earnestly for the faith that was once for all entrusted to the saints. [4] For certain men have secretly slipped in among you – men who long ago were marked out for the condemnation I am about to describe – ungodly men who have turned the grace of our God into a license for evil and who deny our only Master and Lord, Jesus Christ. (Jude 3-4, NET Bible)

[3] For this is the love of God, that we keep His commandments. And His commandments are not burdensome. (1 John 5:3)

The Ten Commandments are not a burden, but keeping them makes one happy.

In this life, God wants us to live successful, happy lives -- to enjoy good health, a challenging career, a beautiful marriage, and happy children. He promises blessings and special protection to those who seek to do His will and keep His commandments!

> [2] Beloved, I pray that you may prosper in all things and be in health, just as your soul prospers. [3] For I rejoiced greatly when brethren came and testified of the truth that is in you, just as you walk in the truth. [4] I have no greater joy than to hear that my children walk in truth. (3 John 2-4)

> [26] "Behold, I set before you today a blessing and a curse: [27] the blessing, if you obey the commandments of the Lord your God which I command you today; [28] and the curse, if you do not obey the commandments of the Lord your God, but turn aside from the way which I command you today (Deuteronomy 11:26-28).

> [19] I call heaven and earth as witnesses today against you, that I have set before you life and death, blessing and cursing; therefore choose life, that both you and your descendants may live; [20] that you may love the Lord your God, that you may obey His voice, and that you may cling to Him, for He is your life and the length of your days; (Deuteronomy 30:19-20)

Living God's way brings a happiness that is more than fleeting pleasure. It brings an assurance when times are rough:

> [13] Happy is the man who finds wisdom, And the man who gains understanding; [14] For her proceeds are better than the profits of silver, And her gain than fine gold. [15] She is more precious than rubies, And all the things you may desire cannot compare with her. [16] Length of days is in her right hand, In her left hand riches and honor. [17] Her ways are ways of pleasantness, And all her paths are peace. [18] She is a tree of life to those who take hold of her, And happy are all who retain her. (Proverbs 3:13-18)

[15] Happy are the people whose God is the Lord! (Psalm 144:15)

[21] He who despises his neighbor sins; But he who has mercy on the poor, happy is he. (Proverbs 14:21)

[14] Happy is the man who is always reverent … (Proverbs 28:14a)

[5] Happy is he who has the God of Jacob for his help, Whose hope is in the Lord his God, [6] Who made heaven and earth, The sea, and all that is in them; Who keeps truth forever, (Psalm 146:5-6)

Living God's way makes us truly happy. We should do that as well as pray for wisdom (James 1:5).

The Ten Commandments were made known to us to help build character in us so that we will be able to be better and make eternity better. We can, in this life, make our own eternity better if we truly trust Him.

Yet, because of distortions from religious leaders, the Apostle Paul was inspired to write about the "mystery of lawlessness" (2 Thessalonians 2:7). According to Jesus, in these end times, lawlessness will increase and cause the love of many to grow cold (Matthew 24:12). Sadly, this will help lead to the final end time "Mystery Babylon the Great" (Revelation 17:5)—a religious power on the city of seven hills (Revelation 17:9,18). For more on that and the Ten Commandments, check out the free online booklet: *The Ten Commandments: The Decalogue, Christianity, and the Beast.*

God's Plan is a Better One

The latter part of God's plan will be better than the first part of the plan as:

[8] The end of a thing is better than its beginning; (Ecclesiastes 7:8)

Yet, notice a contrast between those who doubt God and God's actual people:

> [13] "Your words have been harsh against Me, "Says the Lord, "Yet you say, 'What have we spoken against You?' [14] You have said, 'It is useless to serve God; What profit is it that we have kept His ordinance, And that we have walked as mourners Before the Lord of hosts? [15] So now we call the proud blessed, For those who do wickedness are raised up; They even tempt God and go free.'"
>
> [16] Then those who feared the Lord spoke to one another, And the Lord listened and heard them; So a book of remembrance was written before Him For those who fear the Lord And who meditate on His name.
>
> [17] "They shall be Mine," says the Lord of hosts, "On the day that I make them My jewels. And I will spare them As a man spares his own son who serves him." [18] Then you shall again discern Between the righteous and the wicked, Between one who serves God And one who does not serve Him. (Malachi 3:13-18)

Notice the following prophecy:

> [6] For unto us a Child is born, Unto us a Son is given; And the government will be upon His shoulder. And His name will be called Wonderful, Counselor, Mighty God, Everlasting Father, Prince of Peace. [7] **Of the increase of His government and peace There will be no end**, Upon the throne of David and over His kingdom, To order it and establish it with judgment and justice From that time forward, even forever. The zeal of the Lord of hosts will perform this. (Isaiah 9:6-7)

So, God will increase His government and peace, and there will be no end of that. No end of making things better.

"The apostles, as Jesus had done, proclaimed the gospel — the GOOD NEWS of a coming BETTER WORLD" (Armstrong HW. The Incredible Human Potential. Everest House, 1978).

The coming Kingdom of God is eternal:

> [13] Your kingdom is an everlasting kingdom, And Your dominion endures throughout all generations. (Psalm 145:13)

> [3] How great are His signs, And how mighty His wonders! His kingdom is an everlasting kingdom, And His dominion is from generation to generation. (Daniel 4:3)

> [27] Then the kingdom and dominion, And the greatness of the kingdoms under the whole heaven, Shall be given to the people, the saints of the Most High. His kingdom is an everlasting kingdom, And all dominions shall serve and obey Him. (Daniel 7:27)

Notice that the saints are going to be given an everlasting kingdom. That is consistent with what the Apostle Peter was inspired to write:

> [10] Therefore, brethren, be even more diligent to make your call and election sure, for if you do these things you will never stumble; [11] for so an entrance will be supplied to you abundantly into the everlasting kingdom of our Lord and Savior Jesus Christ. (2 Peter 1:10-11)

Does that mean that we know all the details?

No, but He has given us the ability to grasp and see some of His plans:

> [10] I have seen the God-given task with which the sons of men are to be occupied. [11] He has made everything beautiful in its time. Also He has put eternity in their hearts, except that no one can find out the work that God does from beginning to end. (Ecclesiastes 3:10-11)

> [12] For now we see in a mirror, dimly, but then face to face. Now I know in part, but then I shall know just as I also am known. (1 Corinthians 13:12)

> [9] But as it is written:

"Eye has not seen, nor ear heard, Nor have entered into the heart of man The things which God has prepared for those who love Him." (1 Corinthians 2:9)

So, work is something God wants people to do. God will have those who become His perform works to make eternity better. So we can know part of the plan, and the plan is better than we have understood.

Even in Old Testament times, some glimpsed eternity and the reality of God's plan (cf. Hebrews 11:13-16).

To get an idea of how much better eternity in the Kingdom of God will be compared to "this present evil age" (Galatians 1:4), notice the following:

> [3] And I heard a loud voice from heaven saying, "Behold, the tabernacle of God is with men, and He will dwell with them, and they shall be His people. God Himself will be with them and be their God. [4] And God will wipe away every tear from their eyes; there shall be no more death, nor sorrow, nor crying. There shall be no more pain, for the former things have passed away."
>
> [5] Then He who sat on the throne said, "Behold, I make all things new." And He said to me, "Write, for these words are true and faithful." (Revelation 21:3-5)
>
> [7] ... Everlasting joy shall be theirs. (Isaiah 61:7)
>
> [18] For I consider that the sufferings of this present time are not worthy *to be compared* with the glory which shall be revealed in us. (Romans 8:18)

Not only will there be an end to suffering, there will be real joy. And you can have a part increasing that joy.

7. Concluding Comments

It has been estimated that there has been a total of 40 to 110 billion or so human beings who have lived (and most have died).

Humanity's purpose is not to vainly worship God to accumulate pleasures for ourselves and glory for Him. While eternity will be full of pleasures for us and God is worthy of more glory than we can understand now, our purpose is to make eternity better for others as well.

Jesus has made a place for each of us (cf. John 14:2) as God fashions us individually (Psalm 33:15) to perfect us (Psalm 138:8). He will complete the work He began in each of us who are willing (Philippians 1:6).

The billions of us are all different and have different ways to give. Our ultimate role is to make eternity better--this means that yes, YOU will have a unique way of giving. Unless you ultimately refuse to support God's Kingdom, you will have your part in making eternity better for each and every one of at least 40 billion others and then even more (cf. 1 Corinthians 12:26; Job 14:15; Galatians 6:10)!

The Bible teaches that we are to "esteem others better than" ourselves (Philippians 2:3). Therefore, consider that nearly everyone you ever encountered will one day help make eternity better for you (and you for them). Everyone who you misjudged, been prejudiced against, had wrong thoughts about, perhaps cut-off in traffic, mistreated, as well as those you have been kind to, you may actually have to work for. So try to "be kind to one another, tenderhearted, forgiving one another, even as God in Christ forgave you" (Ephesians 4:32). "As much as depends on you, live peaceably with all" (Romans 12:18).

Since eternity lasts for an infinite amount of time, consider that you will actually be able to know 40 billion (probably more) people much better than you now know yourself!

You may actually have to work for some you felt God could never use (cf. Matthew 21:28-32)—for "many who are first will be last, and the last first" (Mark 10:31).

Consider, further, that the Bible teaches that all people—including those that you may not care much for—have the potential to be filled with all the fulness of God:

> [14] For this reason I bow my knees to the Father of our Lord Jesus Christ, [15] from whom the whole family in heaven and earth is named, [16] that He would grant you, according to the riches of His glory, to be strengthened with might through His Spirit in the inner man, [17] that Christ may dwell in your hearts through faith; that you, being rooted and grounded in love, [18] may be able to comprehend with all the saints what is the width and length and depth and height — [19] to know the love of Christ which passes knowledge; **that you may be filled with all the fullness of God**. (Ephesians 3:14-19).

We are to learn, and to learn more (2 Peter 3:18).

More knowledge was prophesied for the time of the end (Daniel 12:4), including the restoration of things that were lost (Matthew 17:11).

It seems that the knowledge of why God made all that He did is something that needed to be more fully restored.

How does God do that?

> [9] "Whom will he teach knowledge? And whom will he make to understand the message? Those just weaned from milk? Those just drawn from the breasts? [10] For precept must be upon precept, precept upon precept, Line upon line, line upon line, Here a little, there a little." (Isaiah 28:9-10)

> [10] But God has revealed them to us through His Spirit. For the Spirit searches all things, yes, the deep things of God. (1 Corinthians 2:10)

So, by looking at various scriptures, we can learn doctrine. And if we are led by God's Spirit we can understand even more.

And how should individual Christians react when faced with new theological knowledge?

Praying to God for understanding as Job mentioned is one step to take:

> [24] Teach me, and I will hold my tongue; Cause me to understand wherein I have erred. (Job 6:24)

In the New Testament, the Bereans set a noble example:

> [10] Then the brethren immediately sent Paul and Silas away by night to Berea. When they arrived, they went into the synagogue of the Jews. [11] These were more fair-minded {noble, KJV} than those in Thessalonica, in that they received the word with all readiness, and searched the Scriptures daily to find out whether these things were so. (Acts 17:10-11)

Part of the purpose of this book has been to give scriptures so that all who are willing can see that it is so. Part of my purpose in writing it was to share God's truth to all who may have open ears.

God does have a plan for you. God loves you and wants you to love others. You are to live according to His loving way of life. Increasing real love: that can be considered as the meaning of life.

The Bible teaches that the entire creation, including humans, was made "very good" (Genesis 1:31) and that He made and blessed the seventh day (Genesis 2:2-3).

The Bible teaches that although God made humans upright, they have sought many wrong ways (Ecclesiastes 7:29).

Again, please realize that the Bible teaches:

> [8] The end of a thing is better than its beginning; The patient in spirit is better than the proud in spirit. (Ecclesiastes 7:8)

The beginning was very good, and the end will be even better.

God made humanity to reproduce Himself and be part of His family (Malachi 2:15).

He made us to share in His glory (Romans 8:17) and to rule the universe (Hebrews 2:5-17). Jesus taught that, "It is more blessed to give than receive" (Acts 20:35).

God MADE humanity in order to give love (cf. 1 John 4:7-12) and so that there would be more love in the universe (cf. Matthew 22:37-39). That is the meaning of life.

What is the mystery of God's plan? Why did God create anything?

God created what He did so eternity would be better (cf. Hebrews 6:9, 11:16; Philippians 1:23).

That is why He created the universe and that is why He created men and women. He specifically created the universe as a heritage/inheritance for Jesus and all humankind.

Humans who are granted eternal life will make eternity better.

God's plan includes all who will heed His call in this age (see also the free online booklet *Is God Calling You?*), and others in the age to come (see also *Universal OFFER of Salvation, Apokatastasis: Can God save the lost in an age to come? Hundreds of scriptures reveal God's plan of salvation*).

Christian or not, why did God make you?

Your purpose in this life is to build character so you can maximize your potential and increase how much better you can improve eternity.

God made YOU so that you will be able to use your unique talents (Matthew 25:14-23; Luke 19:11-19) to give love in order to make eternity better!

That is why God created what He did. That is why God made YOU.

Continuing Church of God

The USA office of the *Continuing* Church of God is located at: 1036 W. Grand Avenue, Grover Beach, California, 93433 USA. We have supporters all around the world, and in all inhabited continents (all continents, except Antarctica).

Continuing Church of God Website Information

CCOG.ORG The main website for the *Continuing* Church of God, with links to literature in 100 languages.
CCOG.ASIA Asian-focused website, with multiple Asian languages.
CCOG.IN India-focused website, with some Indian languages.
CCOG.EU European-focused website, with multiple European languages.
CCOG.NZ Website targeted towards New Zealand.
CCOGAFRICA.ORG Website targeted towards Africa.
CCOGCANADA.CA Website targeted towards Canada.
CDLIDD.ES This is a totally Spanish language website.
PNIND.PH Philippines-focused website, with some Tagalog.

Radio & YouTube Video Channels

BIBLENEWSPROPHECY.NET Bible News Prophecy online radio.
Bible News Prophecy channel. Sermonettes on YouTube, BitChute, Brighteon, & Vimeo.
CCOGAfrica channel. YouTube and BitChute video messages from Africa.
CCOG Animations Animated messages on YouTube BitChute.
ContinuingCOG & **COGTube**. Sermons on YouTube and BitChute respectively.

News and History Websites

CHURCHHISTORYBOOK.COM Church history website.

COGWRITER.COM News, history, and prophecy website